MODEL MAKING FOR THE STAGE

Keith Orton

The Crowood Press

First published in 2004 by
The Crowood Press Ltd
Ramsbury, Marlborough
Wiltshire SN8 2HR

www.crowood.com

This impression 2008

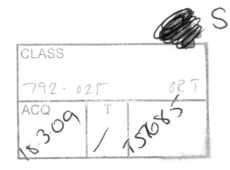

© Keith Orton 2004

British Library Cataloguing-in-Publication Data
A catalogue record for this book is available from the British Library.

ISBN 978 1 86126 690 3

The photographs that accompany each chapter feature productions and students'
work from the Central School of Speech and Drama unless otherwise stated.
The costume in the back cover photo was designed by Jessica Bowles.

Designed and edited by Focus Publishing,
11a St Botolph's Road,
Sevenoaks,
Kent TN13 3AJ

Printed and bound in Spain by GraphyCems, Villatuerta, Navarra

CONTENTS

FOREWORD: THE FASCINATION OF THE MINIATURE

By Tom Piper

This book is a much-needed development for theatre designers at all stages of their careers. For too long, all that has been available are out of date books of the 'build your own stage set' variety, or monographs on established designers. In neither case does a potential designer get a sense of the actual process behind the creation of a design. Keith's book bridges the gap between theory and practice, and places the model at the heart of a designer's creative process.

As with all good teachers, he inspires a quest for quality and imagination, while adding a few helpful shortcuts along the way! There are many ways into the world of theatre design, and I believe that one of its strengths, as an art form in this country, is the varied backgrounds and inspirations of its practitioners. We come from Fine Art, Sculpture, Architecture, Drama, English studies, etc, and in my case even Biology! I only wish that this book had been available when I started out as a largely self-taught designer.

By way of introduction and support to the more detailed analysis and explanation within the book, I would like to illustrate how I

Opposite *Tom Piper's design for* The Tempest *at the RSC. This sequence shows how the set was used to express the devastation of the storm.*

discovered scale model making, and how the model has influenced my design process.

As a child, I was mesmerized by the models in the Egyptian departments of museums: the beautiful model boats that would take the soul of a dead king to the stars, the bakers who would make his bread for the journey, etc. Then, from later eras, other artefacts such as a mechanical tiger eating a man which doubled as a hurdy-gurdy also appealed, as did fantastic early clocks with their workings proudly displayed. All these influences helped to encourage a fascination for making things, creating imaginary worlds and plans for impossible Heath Robinson-esque machines.

In my case, an obsession with tree houses and puppet theatres turned, at university, into the construction of full-scale theatre sets. I had, at that stage, no formal training and didn't even realize that you were meant to make models before embarking on the full-scale build. I worked from sketches, lists of timber lengths and what could be found or recycled from skips; all of which were assembled in seventy-two hours without sleep and then gleefully knocked down again at the end of a production week.

At postgraduate design school, I began to appreciate the value of model making, but, have never forgotten the lessons of working with real materials; appreciating the textures and scale and weight of real stuff. How the world you

Scenographic model of King Lear for the RSC. Designer: Tom Piper

create relates to the scale of the human form, and the exciting possibilities of using found objects in a sculptural way to create an alternative world. The model allowed me the space to experiment, to make mistakes before my ideas became too concrete and public.

Working in Europe has shown me that there is no one fixed way of designing for theatre. The Germans have a superb system called a *Bauprober*, where the ideas from initial rough models are mocked-up with stock flats and timber in the theatre space; this allows you to adjust scale and form in the actual, to view the design from every possible seat, (now possible in a virtual way, too, with 3D modelling) What in a model would have been barely noticeable, a change of height of say 10cm, can have a huge effect on the onstage action.

At the RSC, I managed something similar on a production of *Romeo and Juliet*, adjusting the height of a wall so that the lovers would only just be able to touch fingertips in the balcony scene. We worked out heights using stepladders and string! That knowledge was then brought back to the model and informed its subsequent development.

During my career, I have been lucky to assist Chloe Obolensky on Peter Brooks' production of *The Tempest*. We worked for a month or so, on a model of the Bouffe du Nord in Paris, exploring different ways of reinventing this beautiful 'Empty Space'. All the while the head painter Ulysses worked alongside us, so he was able to explore the way Chloe applied texture and colour, mixing glazes that were then the basis for the painting in the theatre itself. When we moved into the Bouffe du Nord, the model was rapidly set aside as Chloe worked on what was in front of her. The function of the model here was to explore a process of working and to allow the creative team to build up a shared language of expression.

The architect Frank Gehry, of Guggenheim Bilbao fame, uses model making in a wonderfully free sculptural way. Using silver paper, scissors and tape, he and his team rapidly create sketch models. These are photographed and discarded, and the search moves on. Only once he is truly satisfied is a refined model made and scanned used the latest 3D scanner technology: a fine example of how to integrate the necessity of rapid exploration with knowing when is the right time to use computers and current technology to render the final space in detailed model form.

In Britain, we tend to have far shorter preparation and rehearsal times than Europe. The model has, by necessity, become a more crucial means of communication. Designers work as freelancers with many jobs on the go at the same time, and are not on hand to instantly answer every query from the workshops. It is for this reason that we have developed into the world leaders in terms of the finesse of our model making. The delivered model often gives a theatre all the information they need to create the show.

So beware, unless a good relationship is built up with the workshop team – so they understand what is meant to be followed slavishly and what is suggestion or an idea in development – what is put in the model will be what is seen on stage, every nuance or mistake blown up ×25! There is an important balance

to be found, which allows the model to inspire the creativity of fellow craftsmen, rather than giving them complete directions on how to do everything. But, with guidance, debate, references and drawings they understand how the model fits into your personal way of working.

A model, in my view, is one of many tools that a designer uses as a means of expression. It is a way to explore ideas rapidly, to act as the focus of engagement between director and designer. It should never become a holy relic; untouchable because of the hours of labour that have gone into its making or the seductive beauty of its miniature world. What matters is what is on stage, the experience the audience has of the world of the play that your work has helped to evoke. At that point, the model becomes redundant and ends up in a dusty heap on some carpenters bench; its work finished. The final stage production is what matters, not how good the model was.

ACKNOWLEDGEMENTS

There are numerous people whose help and support have been invaluable for the structure, the content and the momentum required for the writing of this book.

Special thanks go to all the staff and students at the Central School of Speech and Drama who have given me the reason to write and the space and the time to make sure that I did, and especially the theatre design students, who, over the last twelve months, have been questioned, photographed and cajoled into contributing to the book, which they did and always with enthusiasm and a sense of pride. I mention here particularly Kerry Shepherd, who made numerous models to highlight certain model-making techniques.

Among the staff, thanks go to Dr Stephen Farrier, who was nearly as excited as I was about the prospect of this book and read it in manuscript with thoroughness and a sense of humour; and to my colleagues Jessica Bowles, Greg Fisher, Sally Mackey, Peter Maccoy, Caroline Miller, Nick Moran, Alistair Noonan, Alex Turnpenny and Rob Pepper, whose knowledge and advice could be bought for the price of a cup of tea or a pint.

Thanks too to the designer Tom Piper for, first, agreeing to write the Foreword, and for then managing to fit the writing of it into an already hectic schedule at the Royal Shakespeare Company.

I include too all the past staff at the Oldham Coliseum theatre who provided me with a secure environment to practise my design and model-making skills, especially the artistic director Warren Hooper, the production manager Phil Clarke, the stage manager Richard Pattison, the resident designers Jackie Trousdale and Celia Perkins, the construction team Steve Kirk, Danny Marsden, Carl Richardson and Jimmie Ragg, and the scenic artist Mathew Jones; Keith Lodwick and the staff at the Theatre Museum in Covent Garden, who helped me to delve into the history of the scenographic model; and Gerry Judah and the staff at the Imperial War Museum for the kind loan of images of the amazing Holocaust exhibition model.

My thanks go also to:
- the 4D Modelshop, 120 Leman Street, London for its support in allowing me to photograph their new premises, even though the staff had barely unpacked.
- the designers Tony Banfield, Paul Botham, Rose Clarke, Phil Engleheart, Richard Foxton, Jacqui Gunn, Nicholai Hart-Hansen, Neil Irish, Simon Kenny, Maira Vazeou, Colin Winslow and Ben Woodgate, each has added his or her personal tips for improving model-making, and very special thanks go to Gary Thorne, who presented me with the opportunity to write this book and has been a constant encouragement.

– Professor Anthony Dean, who was my set design tutor, colleague and all-round model-making guru, introducing me to many the techniques that, through my personal obsession with model-making, have been given the 'Orton' touch.
– the scenic artist and ex-colleague Sue Dunlop, who did not let a little thing like living in Turkey stand in the way of adding her professional expertise and skills to the book.
– and, finally, on a personal note, Mike Bell, whose patience and skills have been crucial to the completion of the book and to keeping me sane!

The scenographic model as presented to the actors: Sylvia's Wedding, *Oldham Coliseum Theatre.*

The final set of Sylvia's Wedding *in its pre-set lighting state (director: Warren Hooper; lighting: Phil Clarke).*

1 INTRODUCTION

Why do designers or model makers put themselves through long hours of intricate and accurate scale model-making? Who is the model for? Is it the most efficient way for them to communicate their design ideas? In the pages of this book are model-making techniques that have been developed over several years of designing and teaching. Some of these relate to the different models that are required within a theatre design process, such as 'sketch models', 'white card models' and the fully finished theatre model known as the scenographic model. Other techniques relate to elements that, together, form a design such as wall and floor treatments, interiors, exteriors and scale figures. Also here are some of the reasons why the scenographic model has remained the favoured method of communicating stage design over the last few decades, and why, even today, with the huge advancement in computer programs and virtual design, it remains so.

Opposite, top *Scenographic model for* Into the Woods.

Opposite, bottom *The two princes played by John Jones and Joe Madison in the finished production of* Into the Woods *(director: Nick Phillips). The quality of the set shows the level of accuracy achieved by the production team in interpreting the model.*

HOW DID THE MODEL AS A DESIGN TOOL COME ABOUT?

The first reference to the use of a design model was in the seventeenth century. Sebastiano Serlio made scale models for proscenium theatre productions where particularly designed flats, backdrops and some architectural structures were required. This model-making was created purely as a guide for the realization of the onstage scenery. Seventeenth-century actors were never expected to respond to the staging but simply perform in front of a scenic background, to interact with the set would have endangered the illusion of scale, depth and perspective that the scenic backdrops were trying to achieve.

The use of the model remained limited throughout the seventeenth and the early eighteenth century. Instead, the preference was for accurate perspective drawings or renderings. Inigo Jones established himself as a great exponent of this method. He brought his experience and knowledge of Italian classical design and, in combination with his love of the English countryside, created his own versions of theatrical masques. The poet Ben Jonson, a contemporary of Jones, highlighted the belief, that the spectacular nature of this masque theatre and its developments in scenery and machinery, were overpowering the production, the words and the actor. This may explain the reason why, as proscenium theatres were growing in popularity and gaining a much wider audience, the staging and scenery became less elaborate and more formulaic and therefore had little need for detailed design models. It was traditional that theatres built up a stock of generic scenery that could be utilized for several productions. Scenery would be mixed and matched making any sense of period or location approximate rather than specific to the requirements of the particular play.

When David Garrick joined the Drury Lane Theatre this tradition began to change. He began commissioning complete new productions and in the 1770s was responsible for employing Philippe Jacques de Loutherbourg, who is credited as the first practitioner to separate the role of design from that of the theatre craftsman.

De Loutherbourg, as a designer, severed the link with the tradition of neo-classical design and used composition and perspective to break with symmetry and create designs that had more naturalism and sense of depth. He did this by creating scale models, which, with associated renderings, supported the work of the constructors and painters. This allowed

Philippe De Loutherburg's model of scenes 1771 and 1785. Photo: Victoria & Albert Museum, London

him time to consider how machinery, lighting and costume interacted with the staging to create a more fluid production. This was revolutionary for its time and De Loutherbourg's fascination with the model led him to create his *Eidophusikon* (literally 'natural form') a fully working, small-scale, model theatre, for which he designed and built complex scenes. Audiences were invited to view these mechanical scenes as an art form in their own right. He was presenting ideas for staging that would be possible only once theatre technology caught up with his vision.

After de Loutherbourg, this separation of roles disappeared again in favour of scene painters such as the nineteenth-century Greive and Telbin families. These craftsmen used scale plans, initial drawings and references from architectural form books to create models comprising backdrops and foreground details for specific proscenium theatres. These models were created to solve the practicalities and choice of colours before starting on the full-scale scenery. They gave themselves, as the scenic artists and the master carpenter, the information needed to create the final set. The use of the model and its construction were beginning to question and challenge the way the stage space was used.

This challenge became more complete with the work of Adolphe Appia and Edward Gordon Craig. At the beginning of the twentieth century these influential practitioners broke with the tradition of design that was trying to recreate reality on stage to move to a much more structural and dynamic expression. Their ideal was to use form, light and the actor to create a performance that allowed staging to be representational rather than to copy real locations. Models became important to both explain intention and experiment during the design and the building process. This gave the opportunity to see how light, now becoming an important factor in the performance, might also sculpt and change the quality of a designed space.

The model has truly taken on a pivotal role as the designer's chosen medium in the last few decades. Once the proscenium arch was broken through, arena stages and experimental studios became the vogue, and designers and directors had more scope to explore the use of space. They could examine how the action within a performance interacted or related to the audience. The three-dimensional scenographic model has given designers the opportunity to collaborate and share their process with other creative people during the design, thereby allowing for a more holistic approach. It has also allowed the designers the opportunity to explore the resonance of the space itself and let this exploration dictate some of the potential lines of enquiry.

WHY THE SCENOGRAPHIC MODEL IS STILL IMPORTANT TODAY

Theatre is about the making of a live event that exists for the duration of each individual performance. Every member of an audience will have his or her own responses and draw conclusions about the performance. The audience are continually discovering the plot through the thoughts and actions of its characters. Therefore one way of looking at scenic design is to see it as another character with its own viewpoint that may confirm or challenge the views of other characters in the play. The discovery of this 'other character' is helped by the manner in which the designer and the director use and experiment with the model. The finished scenographic model stands as a representation of this character in the same way as the other characters exist in print.

Theatre designers tend to enjoy the tactile

Edward Gordon Craig's model for Bach's St Matthew Passion, built 1912–14. This 9ft high model was built from simple sketches with constant, on-going invention. Once finished it was rigged with lights and dimmers for Craig to 'paint' each individual scene with light. Photo: Victoria & Albert Museum, London

qualities that the scenographic model offers them. As they build, select or discard they are manipulating the space with their hands, continually checking scale, space, dynamics and sightlines by moving their head and eyes to change the focal point. This gives the designer an immediate and playful means of exploring a design proposal. No matter how skilled or expert sketches and computer-generated renditions are, they can only ever be a two-dimensional interpretation of a three-dimensional, live event.

*Checking the sightlines.
Student designer Sarah Broad
checking her model of* Guys
and Dolls *from the audience's
perspective.*

It is as a communication tool for the whole production that a scenographic model excels. On its completion, the designer then has to stand before the rest of the production team or the actors and sell the design concept. This gives the designer and the director the opportunity to demonstrate the qualities of the staging by the manner in which they interact and demonstrate the model. These presentations will be nerve-racking but theatrically exciting events. Out front, sitting expectantly, is either the full production team or the freshly formed cast on the first day of rehearsals. It is at this moment that those long hours cutting out bits of card, glueing and painting to get the best possible level of finish and accuracy become worthwhile. The model gives the designer the opportunity to inspire others. It is here that the scenographic model becomes the pivotal piece of communication. It facilitates the move from the drawing board into production.

A scenographic model is a scaled-down proposal. A miniature rendition of what a future audience will see when they attend a live performance. Standing there like a puppet master, the designer reveals scene after scene. By careful selection, the designer can plan and build the model so that its manipulation carries some of the theatricality that will be present when the piece reaches performance.

Something exists in human nature that makes the art of model-making fascinating – we are in awe of the skills and production involving miniaturization. It may provide a link to childhood recollections of dolls' houses, Gulliver and the Lilliputians, or even the Borrowers, but clearly this spell exists. The scale model brings out an almost childlike need to touch and play.

But it is not just the theatre where scale models can have an impact on a selected audience. When architects want to present their concept to others, it is in the form of a 1:100 scale model. This predominantly white-card model is used to bid for the commission or the funding, and once the project has been approved, goes on display to the public to explain how the building will fit in with its surroundings and the community. Another powerful example of a scale model being used to communicate a moment in time is in the Imperial War Museum in London. The museum has a scale model of Auschwitz II-Birkenau death camp, which stretches the entire length of one room of its Holocaust exhibition. The scale and the bleakness of this camp where thousands of Jews arrived by train are evocatively encapsulated in a way that even graphic photographs and the bald facts cannot. It shows over 2,000 Hungarian Jews arriving by trains from the Berehevo ghetto, with a large proportion being separated off and led directly to the gas chambers. This has been painstakingly recreated over two years in 1:100 scale. The detail and characterization within each tiny figure are staggering. Each has its own individuality and, in combination with the enormity of the camp, creates a model that emotionally encapsulates the despair of genocide.

The impressive 1:100 scale model by Gerry Judah of Auschwitz II Birkenau death camp, depicting the arrival of 2,000 Hungarian Jews in May 1944, from the Holocaust Exhibition, Imperial War Museum, London. Photo: Chris King (supplied by G. Judah and the IWM)

WHO IS THE MODEL FOR?

It is important for a designer to remember that, however beautiful and charming the model may be, it is simply a tool within the creative process of making theatre. Of course, after the weeks of experimentation between the designer and the director which led to the preparation of the detailed scenographic model, it would be hard for the designer to then open up the concept to further scrutiny and possible rejection. However, it is important to remember that the model has a purpose beyond the design process; others have to take ownership and responsibility for the creation of the final set, and for them the model will be just as valuable.

The model may go through further stages of development and change once the production team become involved. Scenic artists, constructors and prop makers bring their own skills and needs to the process of constructing the set (known as the build period). It is here that the detail and the level of accuracy that the designer has established in the model-making provide clarity and surety within the build processes.

The model is also used as a basis for costing, so accuracy and an awareness of materials and sheet sizes within the production of the model will provide for more realistic budgeting.

The scenographic model is also crucial to the decisions that a stage management team make. Their only means of preparation before seeing the model will have been script-based. For them it is the opportunity to see how the design works beyond the text, giving them an insight into the quality and the quantity of props and furniture needed. It also provides the spatial information that they need to retain and communicate to the acting company once rehearsals begin.

The stage management will use the model in conjunction with the ground plan to 'mark up' the rehearsal space by laying tape lines on the rehearsal floor that indicate the layout of the set. They need to understand the design fully to know how best to represent it within the rehearsal space. It is their responsibility to remind the director and the actors what the mark-up on the rehearsal floor means in actuality, so that, when the actors get on the set for the first time, their movements and pacing match what they experienced in the rehearsal room.

By the end of the production process, the immaculate scenographic model could return to a designer in pieces, broken up to provide measurements or accurate texture and colour matching. This deconstruction may be crucial in order to obtain the necessary information to make the production true to the designer's intent. A designer must remember that the end of the design process is not the model but the actual, live event.

INSPIRING OTHERS

The designer would hope to build an instant enthusiasm for the design. However, when presenting the model to the production team, a designer will quite often get little or no feedback. This can be quite disturbing and unnerving for a young designer, but remember that the production team will not have been privy to the weeks of experimentation and development that led to the final model. What the designer is showing them is a fully finished design. The production team's minds are often on their own personal role in the production process, analysing the best way to achieve the staging requirements within budget and time constraints. So that it is not surprising that the designer stares out from behind the model at a row of concerned and at times expressionless faces. In time, a designer realizes that this response is a measure of their involvement and not a comment on the quality of the design.

However, when presenting the design to the acting company, the scenographic model generally receives a more positive and verbal reception. It is invariably on the actors' first day of rehearsals: they may have only just met as a company, but are always extremely keen to see how the designer and the director have interpreted the text and how this has manifested itself into a physical proposal for the staging of the production.

Actors often have preconceived ideas about their costumes because they are personal to them and the characters they are building. They rarely feel as qualified to judge the staging proposals in the same way. This again reinforces the notion that the design is another 'character' with which they will interact. They show all those outward signs of enthusiasm and childlike awe towards the model. However, it is also important for the designer to plan this presentation carefully. Making sure that, from this first encounter, the actors gain a clear understanding of the staging implications. They may have less contact with the model once rehearsals start.

The viewing of the model is the only time that the actors see the production from the audience's perspective. Once on stage, their view is quite different: they will see the backs of flats and stage technology, hidden from an audience. So, it is important for them to hold on to a vision of the space as it exists beyond the footlights. It is interesting to observe the number of actors that will physically make contact with the model in this presentation; there is a need to get up close to it, move the figures in the model and handle the furniture. It fulfils a need to play and make personal contact with this miniature version of their acting space.

At the end of the production process it is interesting to observe the number of actors who will comment on the accuracy of the translation from model to stage set, and how much the production team can gain a real sense of pride from being part of this transformation. This reinforces the belief that the scenographic model has a unique communicative role. It truly inspires others to create and participate in the vision that the designer and the director have conceived.

2 GETTING STARTED

INTRODUCTION

The choice of what materials to use for model making is an important one. The process of selection must always consider how a particular material will respond when used to convey scale accurately. To use the same materials as the final product will weaken any sense of scale. When required to convey wood or metal in a model, the use of card, plastics and paint may give a better likeness than actual wood or metal. When making fabrics, drapes and curtains use fine papers, silks or organzas which can be manipulated to create folds and swags. Most other fabrics are too bulky to convey the correct qualities in scale.

Experimentation with different materials will broaden the possibilities available when approaching the crafting of the design model. Different thickness of card, glued and painted, provide not only good facsimiles of walls, doors and floors but also of furniture. Every designer or model maker will have his or her own individual tricks or preferences when choosing

materials for model-making, these are developed through repetition, experimentation and experience.

Most modelling materials can be obtained from general craft shops and DIY stores. Shops selling model railways are a good source of materials for making trees, shrubs and most landscape requirements. There are also specialist model shops which stock complete scale facsimiles of brickwork, floor surfaces, architectural detailing, scale figures and furniture. These shops also sell more specialized model-making equipment such as small-scale lathes.

Opposite *A typical workstation with everything to hand.*

The 4D Modelshop, London, one of the specialist shops selling a full range of model-making equipment and materials.

From Rawlplugs to Theatrical Lights

Look carefully at the different types of plastic plug available in DIY Stores: some have qualities that lend themselves to the creation of scale theatre lanterns. With some minor cuts, sprayed matt back and with the addition of shutters and gels made from thin black card and cellophane, they can be transformed into theatre lanterns. This can be useful when the lighting rig becomes an essential aspect of the design.

The finished theatre lanterns made from Rawlplugs.

Though useful, it is never essential to buy the full range of tools or shop-bought scale facsimiles. Part of the skill and enjoyment of model-making is the discovery of how everyday objects can be adapted to reproduce accurate scale models.

EQUIPMENT

The following provide a useful kit when starting any scale model-making.

Adhesive Tapes
- double-sided tape
- masking tape

Cutting Tools
- craft knife for cutting mountboard and foamboard
- fine handsaw
- pliers with snips
- flat-handled scalpel with 10a or 11 blades for cutting thin card and paper.
- A2-sized cutting mat, self-healing type.

Glues
Clear, general-purpose adhesive; wood glue; PVA; fast-drying, two-part epoxy resin; cyanoacrylate glue; spray adhesive.

The cutting tools and adhesives required when model-making.

Paints, Texture and Sculpting Materials

- selection of watercolour, gouache and acrylic paints
- set of specialist scenic paints (samples), obtained from the scenic suppliers
- selection of emulsion paints, purchased as match-pots in basic colours for scale texturing and the initial blocking of colour
- enamel or acrylic paints (used for plastic kit models), particularly the metallic range
- matt black car spray paint
- modelling putty, either self-drying, epoxy-based or oven-firing
- coloured watercolour pencils
- contour-lining paste in black, white, gold and silver
- gesso or modelling paste for texturing surfaces
- car filler (epoxy-resin variety) for brickwork and flooring.

Brushes

- range of sable or synthetic equivalent watercolour brushes
- fan brush for blending and wood-graining
- stencil brush for stippling and wood-graining.

Other Items and Substances

- scale rule containing 1:10, 1:25 and 1:50 scales for measuring and scaling-down (the three-sided type is easier to use)
- steel rules, 30cm and 60cm, for cutting
- set of compasses with extension bar
- calculator
- broad black permanent marker
- retractable pencil with 0.25 leads in HB and 2H
- small soldering iron with flux and coil solder
- small clamps and sprung tweezers
- fuse wire, piano wire (rigid, strong wire useful for creating flying bars in the model)

Two Cautions

Scalpels are surgical instruments and so can be dangerous if used incorrectly or if their blades are not replaced at regular intervals. Use only for thin card, paper or fine materials. Cuts usually occur when loading or replacing blades or when cutting with a blunt blade where too much pressure has been applied.

Cyanoacrylate glue can bond skin and eyes in seconds. It also requires good ventilation because the fumes are toxic Always read the instructions and warnings carefully before use. Avoid any contact with the skin and apply the glue direct from the nozzle or with the aid of a large dressmaking pin.

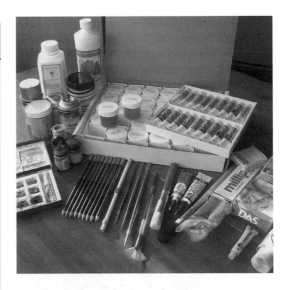

Range of paints, texturing materials and brushes needed for model-making.

- selection of fine sandpapers and emery boards
- matt and gloss clear varnishes
- methylated spirits, turpentine or white spirit.

MATERIALS

Mountboard

Also known as Bristol board, this form of card provides the foundation for much of the structure that is created within the theatre model box. The standard format is approximately A1 and is usually double-sided (colour and white). It ranges in thickness between 1,000 and 1,500 microns. The most often used combination is black and white. This type of card is used throughout the model-making process since it provides strength combined with ease of cutting. It can be used to produce sketch models and white card models and forms a good base for the final model structures that might then be painted or have textures applied. For theatrical masking in the scale model box, a black on black version is available.

Foamboard

This board is available in several thicknesses, the most commonly used being 3mm. Its manufacture provides the perfect qualities for creating the theatre model box and any large structures. Being foam-centred, with a sheet of thin card on both sides, it is both rigid and lightweight. Most commonly available in white, it may also be obtained in black. It is important to remember that aerosol paints and certain glues will attack the foam infill and so should be avoided.

Ticket Card

The name ticket card indicates the type of card that is normally used for business cards and invitations. It may not be labelled as such in art shops and so any of the art cards that are of six-sheet thickness will be suitable. It is available in a wide range of colours, of which black and white are the most useful. It has a hot-pressed surface that will take paints and other media without warping, and it forms a good base structure for curved elements of staging, furniture and fine detailing within the structure of the model.

Paper

It is useful to collect interesting varieties of paper and thin card. Some manufacturers will send out samples of their ranges in swatchbooks that provide a range of colours, thicknesses and textures. A supply of plain cartridge paper is useful for sketching out ideas and producing quick options for sketch models that can be cut out with scissors. Tracing paper and graph paper are required for technical drawing and also pattern making for certain model making options.

Some handmade papers sold as gift wrapping can provide the basis for natural landscape flooring or heavily textured walls. Tissue paper is useful for clothing scale figures and by soaking it in a mixture of PVA and water it is possible to create drapes and textured surfaces.

Acetate Sheeting

Use clear acetate sheets to create glass for windows and doors. Collect clear plastic packaging for creating modern fixtures and fittings. For example, the ridged side panels of sandwich packs, when cut to size, will create 1:25-scale radiators.

Brass or Copper Sheeting and Tubing

These can be purchased from craft DIY shops or by mail order and can provide the structuring for fretwork and metal framework.

Even if the metal finish required is of a type other than brass or copper, it is better to use these since they solder easily and can then be painted to create the required metallic finish.

Thin Balsa Wood and Veneers

There are occasions when real wood may be useful, particularly for rustic furniture and items such as fences and gates. Fine-grain veneers can be cut up to create patterned block flooring where several colours of wood are essential. Balsa wood is easily to cut or carved for flat areas of staging. However, it is not so useful for self-standing furniture as it becomes extremely brittle when one tries to create spindles and legs.

Sheet, Tube and Rod Plastics

These can be purchased from specialist model shops and moulded easily or cut with a craft knife when heat is applied. Use plastic for its own visual quality or as an alternative to mountboard when making small detailed structures. Tube and rod can be useful for pillars and columns.

When approaching each new design, the model-maker will have to consider the merits of each surface or structure within the final scenographic model. Until faced with a particular challenge, the designer/model-maker may not have available an appropriate process for the construction of an item – it is the model-making problem that drives the enquiry. Every designer develops personal methods and techniques, but the real skill is in analysing and discovering the potential that a material has for conveying scale, purpose and finish. It is the experimentation and striving for perfection that establishes true model-making quality, and this is achievable with even the most basic of materials and equipment.

THE LAYOUT OF THE WORKSTATION OR STUDIO

Before beginning any model-making, spend some time making sure that the working space is safe and suitable for the tasks ahead. It is useful to have a workstation that has a solid, stable desk or table with an adjacent wall for pinning up reference images, sketches or plans. Make sure that this surface is big enough to allow the cutting of A1 pieces of board.

Choose the right chair: a designer/model-maker spends long hours making models, so make sure that the chair is comfortable, has a back support and is of the right height for the worktable. An office type of chair, with swivel castors, can allow for ease of movement between the worktable and the model.

A sculpting stand can be useful to position alongside the workstation to build the model box on. This means that it can be separate from the modelling area and be set at a viewing height similar to the audience's sightlines. This will allow for constant checking and evaluating during model-making and help to avoid blocking and unexpected scale discrepancies.

Make sure that you have good lighting. It is important that, wherever possible, this is overhead to prevent shadows being cast across your work when using steel rules and scalpels. An anglepoise lamp with a base or clamp will give you directional light for close work. It also provides a useful means of playing with light during the experimental stages of designing and offers the opportunity to discuss lighting ideas with the director and the rest of the design team.

Use a metal bin for the disposal of rubbish. This is preferable since most materials used are inflammable and, should an accident occur, the fire can be contained and extinguished more easily in such a container.

25

Because of the constant need to refer to and to draft plans and working drawings, a drawing board, preferably with parallel motion is required. This could be self-standing or a table-top variety, but should be A1 in size to accommodate the standard sizes of theatre ground plans and section views. It is useful to have these plans taped to the drawing board. This allows for constant reference, such as design ideas drawn direct on the plans or positioning pieces of the model to check scale and fit during the assembly of the model.

A computer (laptop or desktop) connected to a scanner and printer has now become a useful tool for the designer and model-maker. Images can be scanned, downloaded and manipulated to create the initial design renderings, working drawings, storyboards or even the surfaces used direct in the scenographic model itself.

To spend time and money getting a workstation laid out properly will make the model-making process more efficient. When working to deadlines it is useful to know that everything is to hand, that time will not be lost rushing out to buy extra items or in searching under piles of paper and materials.

WORKING TO DEADLINES

It is important to ascertain from the beginning of the project what the deadlines are. The theatre will have set the production dates, a cast and technical staff may have been employed, the first day of rehearsals has been set. These are all immovable. The design and the finished model have to meet the deadline or every other aspect of the production process will be delayed. Therefore, to allay some of this pressure, it is important to analyse how much time there is available for design and model-making. Try not to edit down the experimental stage of the process. When time is limited, there is a tendency to want to rush into making the final model too soon. This can cause creative blocks and indecision through a lack of understanding of the possibilities that the design has to offer. Experimentation leads to a confidence in knowing the subject and exactly what needs to be made and why it is right.

The final scenographic model will always take longer to complete than has been estimated. Even experienced designers and model-makers can get caught out. The time needed will obviously depend on the complexity of the design; as a guideline, allow two weeks to work solely on the construction of the finished model. Even if everything has been worked out and the design has been thoroughly tested and approved, there will always be more problems to solve.

The process usually breaks down into three interrelated sections needing equal emphasis:
- text analysis and research;
- experiments with the space and design (sketch and white-card models);
- creating the scenographic model.

Each should have approximately the same amount of time allocated to it. So, taking the example of a two-week period for constructing the finished model, an ideal design process should be given at least six weeks for its completion. But there will be occasions when the time available is not ideal, when the designer has less time in which to complete the task. Then the choices are:
- work longer hours to achieve the result;
- employ an assistant to help with model-making;
- turn down the job!
  Equally difficult can be having too much time. This can lead to:
- delay in starting due to lack of urgency;
- spending too long experimenting with ideas, creating too many options;
- over-analysing or ignoring personal, gut feelings.

Using 1:50 scale to create a scenographic model (for Blood Brothers, *Haymarket Theatre, Coventry) that makes transporting the model much easier (designer: Anthony Dean; director: Warren Hooper).*

A designer will eventually discover a timescale that best suits him or her. To manage stress levels is important, but to avoid stress is unlikely. There seems to be a definite synchronicity between reasonable pressure and creativity in theatre. Remember, when meeting deadlines, the designer is not carrying the burden alone, there is a creative team, including the director and other designers, to share the responsibility.

TECHNIQUES

Measuring

There are several appropriate scales to bear in mind when considering building scale models for theatre: 1:10, 1:25, 1:50 and 1:100. The choice depends on the size of the theatre and the purpose of the model.

1:10 Scale

When elements of the staging are complicated or detailed a larger scale may be required to communicate fully the information necessary for its build or decoration. This is also a useful size when preparing maquettes of puppets, intricate props and costume props.

1:25 Scale

This is the standard used for the majority of scenographic models. It has been the accepted scale to use and stems from imperial measurements, where $\frac{1}{2}$in represented 1ft (1:25 being the metric equivalent). This scale allows enough accuracy and detail for the needs of all departments for both creating the staging and producing a mark-up in the rehearsal room.

1:50 Scale

This scale is used for larger theatre venues where 1:25 would prove too big to model or transport. It may also be a useful scale in which to prepare sketch or white-card models before completing a final 1:25 version. Some designers prefer to work in this scale for all finished models; although quicker to model, it may be difficult to achieve the level of accuracy and detail that communicates all the necessary information for the building and painting of the final set. However, it can be useful if the model has to tour with the production where it will be used as a guide for each fit-up.

1:100 Scale

Used for finished models where the scale of the venue is vast or for quick sketch models where several design possibilities can be explored while avoiding an over-attachment to one particular idea. It is also the standard scale used by architects for presentation models to provide an artist's impressions of the finished structure and its surroundings.

Using the Scale Rule

Scale rules can be purchased that contain all of these scales on the one rule, but check to make sure that this is the case before purchasing one from an art shop. To convert to any selected scale is as easy as measuring with a standard rule; thus, if drawing a character shape in 1:25 scale while the actual size of the figure is 1.5m, find the 1:25 scale, on the rule simply mark a point at the beginning of the scale and then check along the rule to find where 1.5m is marked and make a second point. It is an automatic conversion. Similarly, if you want to know what something is in 1:25 scale then simply measure it with the edge of the rule marked 1:25. The measurement reading will be in full-scale metres and centimetres. Calculate any scale in the same way. For 1:10 and 1:100 you can use an ordinary metric rule, but it makes sense to use the scale rule when carrying out any scale conversion. This allows for constant comparison between the model and what is meant in actuality.

Cutting

Have a cutting mat placed on the worktable at all times and avoid cutting on the surface of the table or using scraps of card. The self-healing type of mat will make sure that each cut is against a clean surface, with no chance of the blade following previously cut lines.

Always use a steel rule when cutting. Check that it has a cork backing; if not, fasten a piece

Using a scale rule to check the measurement of an item of set in 1:25 scale.

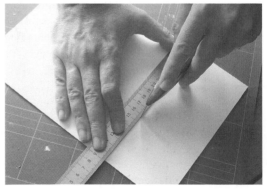

Cutting mountboard with a craft knife, showing the correct position for holding both the rule and the knife.

of masking tape along its length since this will help to stop the rule from slipping during the cutting. Choose the appropriate type of cutting knife. The broader type of craft knife is best suited to foamboard, mountboard, plastics and veneers. Use a scalpel for ticket card, paper, thin acetate sheeting and balsa wood.

Bear in mind how old the blade is or how much use it has had. When a blade begins to catch or it takes an increased pressure to cut through, then change the blade. This will create sharper and cleaner cut edges and prevent the need to make several attempts at cutting through the material.

When cutting make sure that you position yourself above the cut line so that you can see the edge of the rule and the blade line clearly. This will also mean that your weight is positioned properly. Place the tips of your fingers on the centre of the rule well away from the edge. Position the blade on the line and then move the rule up to the side of the blade. Check that the blade is vertical. When cutting, apply gentle pressure to the knife and cut downwards and away from the body. Certain materials may need more than one pass with the knife. Do not be tempted to move the rule until you are sure that you have cut right through. There is a different feel when the blade is cutting into the surface of the mat. Be aware of this change to know that the cut is complete.

Joining

When choosing which adhesive to use, check the packaging or the tube to discover which type is best suited to the materials you want to join. Read all directions carefully, especially any hazard warnings. The following are suggestions to aid the selection process.

1. Clear, multipurpose adhesives are versatile since they will join card, balsa and certain plastics, they are readily available, dry

Injection Glueing

To make the use of clear adhesives more controlled use a hypodermic syringe. These can be purchased cheaply from any chemist (the 10ml ones are a convenient size). The needles (which come separately) are colour-coded according to diameter; the white ones are the best for most needs. Snip off approximately half of the needle point so that you have a 'square-cut' end (*ensure that all cut-off points are disposed of very carefully*). Put some adhesive into the syringe, invert it and squeeze out the air bubbles, just as medical professionals do, and insert a pin into the needle end to prevent the glue from hardening when it is not in use. By using a syringe you can carefully control the amount of glue that is being applied and avoid messy joins.

completely clear (glossy) and allow time for realignment; however, the adhesive can emerge of the tube too quickly and can be difficult to control; if this is a problem, squeeze a small amount on to a piece of scrap card and apply it to the surfaces to be joined with the head of a dressmaking pin or a cocktail stick; it dries quickly so hold the materials in place until it has hardened.

2. Another option for joining card is to use PVA or wood glue. These adhesives have a longer drying time but can provide cleaner and stronger joins. Apply the glue evenly to both surfaces, leave for 30sec for it to go tacky before joining. Hold in position until the adhesive has hardened. When glueing foamboard to itself or card, push dress-making pins through the join to hold it in place until the glue has hardened.

3. Epoxy adhesive can be used to join wood,

29

hard plastics, thin metal sheeting, small gauge metal rod or bar. Make sure that it is the rapid drying variety. With this adhesive it is important that you have the correct mixture. Carefully squeeze out equal lengths from the two tubes supplied and mix thoroughly, apply thinly and evenly to the two surfaces and allow 30sec before joining them. The adhesive will harden in $\frac{1}{2}$–1hr and so the join may need to be clamped or held together with tape. Remove any excess of glue with a scalpel.

4. A contact adhesive can be useful when joining plastics and foam because other types of adhesive may react and dissolve the surface. The trick with contact adhesive is to leave it for a full 10min after its application before the joining; the surfaces will appear almost dry to the touch. Then carefully position and bring the surfaces together, as soon as they touch the join will be instantaneous and permanent.

5. Cyanoacrylate glue will join a wide range of materials instantly. Follow the instructions carefully because it can bond skin in seconds. Use this glue for the intricate joining of plastics or metals, for example, beads. Always use tweezers and never touch the join until you are sure that it has hardened.

6. Adhesives intended especially for model-making can be obtained from specialist retailers. Although expensive, they are made to deal with the intricacies of small-scale joining and come with fine nozzles to make their application easier.

7. There is also a specialist product known as 'plastic welding', which, as its name suggests, will join plastics in a strong, clean bond. Two chemicals are applied, one to each plastic surface. When the two surfaces are brought together a reaction bonds the plastics immediately and permanently.

Joining Two Pieces of Card to Form a Right-angled Corner

Apply adhesive to the edge of one of the pieces of card, making sure that no adhesive gets on to the outside surface. Pick up the other piece and bring its edge into contact so that the join is just touching on the outside but open at an angle of approximately 135 degrees. Close the two pieces together to form the right angle. Spare adhesive will be pushed inside the angle, leaving a clean corner free from any surplus.

Joining two sides of a box, showing the angle and the method of glueing that pushes the surplus glue away from the outside fascias.

Exercise: Creating a Perfect Black Cube

To practise measuring, cutting and joining, make a black cube from mountboard. This should be an exact 2m cube in 1:25 scale. Form the cube by joining six separate faces. This will employ the use of:

- a scale rule and set square to mark out each face, remembering to allow for the thickness of the card in the measurement and assembly;
- a craft knife and steel rule for cutting out each individual face;
- glueing techniques to make sure that the outside surfaces of the cube are completely free from adhesive.

If, at any stage, the faces are not accurately cut or glue is visible, start again. When you are completely satisfied, use a black marker and carefully colour in the white edges that are visible. This exercise will help you to practise these skills and instil a need for accuracy and neatness.

Complete the black cube by carefully joining the last side and make sure that the adhesive does not spread to the outside by applying it only to the underside of the last fascia.

Soldering

Small-scale soldering is a useful technique to develop and use when there is a need to create any metal structures within the scenographic model. A small stick soldering iron, solder and flux can be purchased from any DIY store. To solder any two metals together you must first consider the type or types of metal: galvanized and most general-purpose wires are impossible to solder efficiently or neatly. For the best results use copper or brass as they are good heat conductors.

Cut the metal to the correct lengths and position it so that the two sections are touching. Do this by pushing the pieces into two small blocks of modelling clay or foamboard, leaving as much distance as possible between the supporting material and

Exercise: Creating a Scale Chair by Soldering

Practise soldering techniques by making a simple metal frame chair in 1:25 scale. Use the 1:25-scale diagram shown as a pattern. With a small set of long nose pliers bend and cut the copper or brass wires to fit the individual pieces. To straighten wire that has been on a spool, apply tension to both ends with two sets of pliers. The stretching of the wire will cause a reaction in the metal and the wire will become perfectly straight. Follow the instructions for soldering. The design of this chair allows for the assembly of all the sections of the frame in one procedure. Once soldered, remove the chair from the foamboard support and paint or spray the frame silver. Make the seat and the back rest from black mountboard cut to the sizes indicated in the diagram and glue to the frame with cyanoacrylate glue. The chairs can be used to create the audience seating in a scenographic model since the process is so quick.

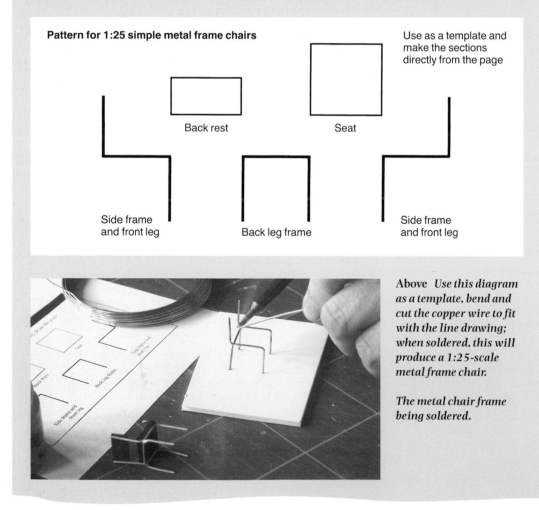

Pattern for 1:25 simple metal frame chairs

Use as a template and make the sections directly from the page

Back rest

Seat

Side frame and front leg

Back leg frame

Side frame and front leg

Above *Use this diagram as a template, bend and cut the copper wire to fit with the line drawing; when soldered, this will produce a 1:25-scale metal frame chair.*

The metal chair frame being soldered.

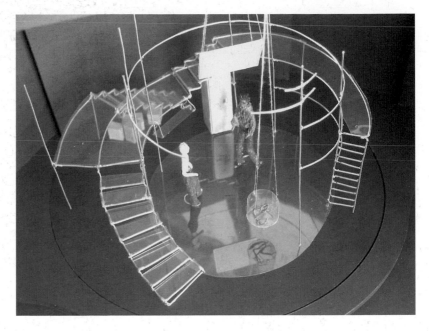

Right *A design model that has employed soldering techniques to create the scaffolding and treads (for* Snake in the Fridge; *student designer: Lesley Read).*

the join. Then anchor the modelling clay or foamboard to the work surface. Make sure that the pieces are at the correct angles in the vertical and the horizontal plane. With a cocktail stick, apply a small amount of the flux to the area of the join. Take the soldering iron and burn the flux away by resting the fully heated tip against the join. It is important to include this preparatory stage since the burning of the flux cleanses the join while the soldering iron is heating up the pieces of metal. Take 1mm-gauge solder and carefully bring it

together with the heated metal joint. Allow at least 1min for the join to cool down. The modelling clay will begin to warm up the more soldering you do; if it does, use a refrigerator for a few minutes to firm it up. *Do not heat the solder with the iron.* Remember that it is the heated joint that melts the solder, not direct contact with the soldering iron. Use the soldering iron correctly and the solder will run neatly into the join, use it badly and the solder will stick to the iron and create a messy joint.

3 TECHNIQUES FOR CREATING SURFACES AND TEXTURES

INTRODUCTION

One of the strengths that a scenographic model has over any renderings or computerized images is the dimensional qualities of its surface textures. Whether this is brickwork, stone, metal, wood or glass, the finish that the designer or the model-maker presents contains his or her personal choices and individual style. It may take several hours to achieve just the right balance of colour or sense of decay or ageing, some may even be lucky accidents, but, once completed, the surface or texture creates a clear statement of intent for the final production.

It will be the scenic artist's job to interpret these surfaces, so where possible it is useful to use some of the same materials and techniques that they will employ, only miniaturized. This will aid them in achieving the quality and the level of finish that the designer wants. These techniques include paintwork, marbling, brickwork, wood graining and metalwork. The clearer the

Opposite *A section of a model showing a rusted metal texture formed by using scrunched black tissue paper pasted on to mountboard and then rubbed into with a copper-coloured framing paste (for* Sweeney Todd; *director: John Abulafia).*

scenographic model, the more focused the sampling becomes, allowing the scenic artists the time in which to refine the finish rather than to spend time on random sampling.

To provide this level of accuracy the designer/model-maker must understand the exact qualities of the materials they are suggesting. If the surfaces are copies of real materials, then it is essential to work from either good quality photographic images or the actual material itself. If the surface is a creative interpretation, then the scenic artist will still need to know the design influences or references that the designer has used to be able to recreate the designer's request.

When creating a surface texture or colouring, keep a log of how you achieved the effect together with a sample sheet of the base material and the colours used. This will be a useful personal reminder for recreating the treatment again and a key for the scenic artists to sample from. It may even avoid the need to dismantle the model for colour-matching purposes. On small-scale productions, the designer may also be painting the finished set, which makes it even more important to discover the necessary information during the model-making process.

The following are examples of how to achieve different textured surfaces in 1:25 scale. Use the same methods in 1:10 scale, but the sizes and some textures will need to

35

A brick wall made by scoring into the surface of foamboard with a scalpel, then spray painted in matt black.

increase proportionately. With 1:50- or 1:100-scale models some of these techniques are too intricate.

BRICKWORK

Brickwork will take many forms in modelling for theatre. Most backstage areas and some studio spaces are brick-built. To get a good sense of reality in a theatre model box, it is often useful to recreate this brickwork; this may be done in the following two ways.

Bricking Large Areas of the Stage Space

When creating any brickwork it is essential to know the measurement of the individual bricks. They differ in proportion, depending on their make. When first attempting brickwork, measure and mark out the pattern before cutting. Later, with experience, this stage can be excluded and the pattern created by eye.

If the walls of a theatre model box are made from foamboard there is a quick and effective method for creating brickwork. Take a sharp scalpel and score into the foamboard, approximately one-third of its thickness; the horizontal lines then represent the mortar

between rows of bricks. Score in the verticals, following the pattern for the particular style of brickwork. As the vertical cuts are made, the foamboard will both indent and randomly bow to create a more naturalistic effect. Then spray paint matt black; this gives a neutral black finish that highlights the brickwork pattern. It is best to take the process to this stage even if eventually the brickwork is painted a different colour to match the design requirements. The second method is to buy scale brick from a specialist model store. This comes in plastic sheeting that is easily cut with a scalpel to any size required. Remember to cut around the pattern rather than through the bricks when joining sheets together. In this way, once the sections are matched, glued down and painted, the join will be invisible.

Brick Walls or Floors within the Design

Where there is a need to create a particular quality, of either a specific make, ageing or even crumbling brickwork, then the following methods are better options.

Epoxy-filler Brickwork
This method closely resembles the way scenic

artists create specific brickwork by applying a textured medium through a stencil. Because of the materials used in this procedure, make sure that this process is done in a well-ventilated room. Take the section of the 1:25 model that requires brickwork and position it on a cutting mat. With a 2H pencil and a set square draw on the grid for the brickwork. Then tear off strips of masking tape of double the width of the section you are making and lay them out, sticky side down, on the cutting mat. Take a scalpel and a steel rule and cut this masking tape lengthways into 1mm strips. Lift these off the board and position them along all the horizontal lines. Make sure that each masking tape strip is centred so that a quarter of the tape is overhanging at each end, which may be lightly tacked to the cutting mat.

Then tear off further full strips of masking tape, this time equal to the height of the section of walling. Repeat the same procedure as before to create 1mm strips of masking tape. Fasten these, following the vertical pencil lines, over the horizontal tapes. Although the drawn vertical lines alternate between rows, ignore this fact and run the tape strips up the entire height. The result will be a squared-up grid of masking tape over the whole area, rather than a brick pattern.

To regain the brick pattern, carefully cut away every other vertical masking tape strip, line by line. Do this by cutting inside the horizontal masking tape strips, so that each individual vertical strip remains overlapping a horizontal. Remember to alternate between each line that is cut to create the brick pattern, and not a stack effect. On a separate piece of card, mix up more than enough epoxy car filler to cover the entire surface of the wall. Squeeze out equal lengths from the two tubes and mix thoroughly with the plastic spreader provided. The reason for overestimating the quantity is that the product has a quick drying time

(approximately 3min before it is unworkable) and this process has to be completed in one application.

Once thoroughly mixed, take the spreader with some of the epoxy filler and draw it lightly across the grid of masking tape. Be careful not to spread it too thickly nor too forcefully; the covering should be thin enough for you to see the masking tape faintly underneath. Work quickly and repeat the action until the whole section is complete. At this stage, a small sponge may be used to roughen the surface to create a greater sense of decay, or it may be left untouched to create clean, smooth brickwork.

Before the epoxy filler has completely set,

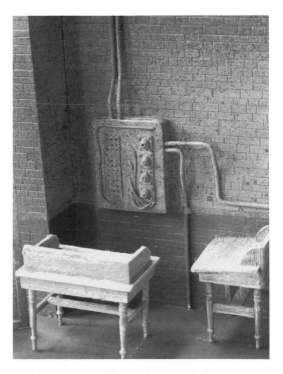

Section of a model showing the use of shop-bought brick sheeting assembled and painted to recreate a backstage setting for **Mephisto** *(designer: Anthony Dean).*

Cutting away alternate, vertical strips of masking tape to create the brick pattern.

Applying a thin coat of mixed epoxy filler with a plastic spreader.

Carefully peeling back the masking tape grid to reveal the bricks and mortar lines.

The finished epoxy filler bricks painted and used in various ways to create an outside wall and doorway (student designer: Sara Svensson).

gather up one side of the horizontal strips of masking tape and carefully and slowly pull across and way from the surface of the walling. The masking tape will lift past the epoxy filler and leave clear mortar lines between the epoxy-filler bricks. Leave this to harden fully before painting. If some of the vertical strips of tape remain in the filler, these can be plucked out by using the tip of the scalpel blade.

The surface is now finished and ready for painting. If dark, old mortar is required, then rub the colour into the gaps with paint on a damp rag. Rubbing the colour into the surface of the bricks themselves also highlights the contours that the epoxy filler has naturally developed. If the surface of the bricks is too rough, then smooth this out with sandpaper of a fine grade.

This technique relies on confidence and practice to get the timing right. Experiment on scraps of card before tackling an actual section of model.

Cut Paper Method

Look for a paper that has a definite, coarse structure that echoes the texture of brick when reduced to 1:25 scale; use coarse-grade watercolour paper or a suitable handmade paper. Pre-paint the paper to the right colour and ageing that is required by building up washes of colour with either specialist scenic paint, gouache, watercolour paints or a combination of all three. When you are satisfied, cut the paper into 300mm lengths that are of the equivalent width of double-sided tape. Cut a 300mm length of the tape and apply it to the back of one of the strips of pre-painted paper. Place a section on a cutting mat and, with a scalpel and a steel rule cut a strip off that is the equivalent to the depth of a scale brick. With a 2H pencil, mark this strip into brick lengths. With a scalpel, carefully cut through the paper but not the backing of the double-sided tape to provide a strip of individual bricks still held together by the backing tape.

39

Take a new sheet of coloured paper that has been painted to match the colour of the mortar and, with a 2H pencil, draw a fine line across the paper which is the same depth from the top as the depth of the brick strip that has just been made. Take the strip and, with the scalpel point, pluck off the first brick and position it on the line. The other bricks should peel off easily and be applied to create the brick pattern; remember to allow a 1mm gap for the mortar lines. To vary the quality and the colour of adjacent bricks rotate the strips. Repeat down the sheet of paper, remembering to leave 1mm gap between rows.

It is a good idea to make up an A4 sheet or sheets of this brickwork and cut out sections of the sheet as required. Join them by using the same method as that suggested for bought plastic sheets. Keep any spare walling in A4 plastic sleeves labelled with the design or the type of brick and keep these in a file for future use.

To fasten this brickwork to the required section of walling use spray adhesive. Once assembled, add any further colour or ageing. Use a light dusting of matt black car-spray paint to break down the painted surfaces and add a final degree of ageing. Where a wall is crumbling and falling away, the modelling of individual bricks may be necessary. Make these with modelling putty and, once they have dried, glue them into place with a mixture of PVA and plaster. Paint them with the same colours to blend in with the rest of the wall.

These examples will also apply to 1:10 scale. If textured brick walls are required at 1:50 or 1:100 scale, then apply a coating of modelling paste and score mortar lines in using the point of an old compass, or the mortar lines may simply be drawn in with a 2B pencil or a chinagraph pencil.

PAVING

For most forms of paving, such as slabs, slate or stone floors the same techniques already discussed for brickwork can be adopted. It is useful to add a glaze made from equal parts of PVA and water to create the slight sheen that well-worn floors have. To create an even more accurate slate floor, use the cut paper method and add several contour layers of pre-coloured paper to recreate the fractured quality that exists when slate is formed.

To create a stone floor that is uneven and

Paving created by applying household filler to a plywood base and scoring the paving stones into the filler while it is wet (student model-maker: Eve Lowrie; model of the Minack Theatre, Cornwall).

Rubbing gouache paint into a prepared plaster wall to create an aged and weathered quality.

worn down by centuries of use, cut out individual stone tiles in mountboard. Apply a surface layer of air-drying sculpting putty to the card and mould to give the right effect (at least 2mm thick), then set it aside to dry. Once dry, the tile will usually part easily from the mountboard; then assemble the putty tiles to create the flooring required. To refine the fit or build in more wear, fine sandpaper and emery boards will prove useful. The tiles may even be broken up and assembled to create a damaged floor. Once complete, the floor may be coloured by using acrylic paints and given its final glaze. The use of terracotta-coloured sculpting putty will reduce the time needed to create a terracotta-tiled floor.

PLASTERED WALLS

At 1:25 scale, one of the best and simplest methods is to use household emulsion paint. Because of the variety of shades available and the small quantities that will be needed, buy only the small match pots sold as samples at any DIY store. Adjust the colour to get an exact match by adding either specialist scenic paint or gouache. For an aged plaster, apply the emulsion unevenly. When it has completely dried, rub a darker shade of the same colour into the crevices of the surface with a dab of gouache paint on a damp rag. Make changes to the texturing by stroking the surface with a clean, damp rag to reveal the base colour. This will give highlights within the plaster and create a sense of depth. Because emulsion paint is waterproof when dry, it is possible to correct treatments by cleaning off the paint and starting again.

For very rough, plastered walls, apply modelling paste or gesso with a small modelling trowel to the surface of the board. Use the trowel to get the effect required. Allow it to dry, then use emulsion paint in the same way as before. Remember, when using gesso that the material shrinks as it dries. The texture will have to be more exaggerated to allow for the shrinkage and flattening that will occur.

41

Preparing wood-grain samples (scenic artist: Sue Dunlop).

WOOD-GRAINING

It is difficult to find actual timber that will give accurate wood-graining at 1:25 scale. Some veneers obtained from specialist model shops may be suitable, depending on the required finish and the size of graining in relation to the scale item. However, it unlikely that scenic departments will use expensive timbers within

the build of the final set, it is much more likely that they will use their skills to create paint effects that both match and theatrically heighten the qualities of the required timber.

Scenic artists use a large number of different methods, brushes and tools to create wood-grain effects. With all wood-graining what is important is the research and preparation. Wood-graining can be a good indicator of period; different timbers were available and used at different periods in history. The cut of the timber was important to carpenters and cabinetmakers too: they chose different cuts across the grain to achieve different effects. Make sure that these details are researched thoroughly to provide the correct period and methods of manufacture. Find samples of the actual timber or good photographic references to produce accurate facsimiles of particular types or variations of timber.

Colour Matching for Different Timbers
To get the right qualities of the several timbers it is important to get the base colour and top coats correct and subsequent washes of the right colour and consistency.

Apply the appropriate base colour to the mountboard, using a small roller to eliminate brush marks. To get a really smooth quality of finish, apply one coat, allow it to dry, then sand with fine grade sandpaper before applying a

Colour Matching for Different Timbers

Timber	Emulsion Base Colour	Colour Wash Using Specialist Scenic Paint
mahogany	nectarine	mix of burnt umber and black
oak	bamboo	mix of yellow ochre, black and burnt umber
pine	cameo	mix of raw sienna, burnt umber and black
walnut	cinnamon	mix of Vandyke brown, burnt sienna and black
maple (bird's eye)	parchment	mix of raw sienna, raw umber and burnt umber

second coat. The smoother the finish, the better the graining will be. It is important to get the base colour correct because it will show through the colour washes.

Mahogany

Mix the colour wash (using the colours listed) together with a delaying agent and water to the consistency of milk. Dampen the surface of the base-coloured board with a wet brush. With a medium watercolour brush, apply the colour wash randomly across the damp surface, leaving some areas of base colour showing. Draw a clean, dry brush vertically down the board to create the vertical graining consistent with mahogany timbers. Before the paint has completely dried, blend the lines by drawing a small fan brush through the paint surface at 90 degrees to the vertical stripes.

By applying the colour wash at different angles the different types of grain can be achieved, such as a swirling grain that tends to run diagonally across or a crotch figure, where two curved diagonals join to form a symmetrical pattern. If the pattern becomes too formal then apply water on a clean brush to help to merge and alter hard lines. Blend these by using the fan brush.

When the paint dries, the colour appears flatter and duller. Use a PVA glaze or wood-stain varnish to bring the contrast and colours back. Add colour to the glaze if the colour needs to be adjusted.

Oak

There is not just one type of oak: it appears as light, mid or dark. When mixing the colour wash different quantities of each colour will replicate the different types. Mix in water and a delaying agent so that the colour wash has the consistency of single cream. Test the colour on a sample board painted with the base colour until the colour is a correct match.

There are different effects that occur as oak

grows that help to signify this particular timber. These are flashings (small diagonal flecks of light that run diagonally across the timber), a fine vertical grain and broader contour graining, where branches have shifted and distorted the growth rings.

Dampen the base-coloured board with a wet brush and begin applying a wash with a small household paintbrush, keeping the brush strokes in one direction. To create the flashing flecks use a very fine, dry brush and remove the paint revealing the base colour. Then take a soft stencil brush and gently pat the side of the brush against the colour wash, working vertically up the board. This will produce the fine vertical grain. This process is called

A designer using scenic art techniques to create a 1:10-scale version of wood-graining for model-making purposes (student designer: Tracey Cliffe).

43

'flogging' and echoes the technique that the scenic artist uses.

Once this has dried, add the growth-ring contour graining by mixing a slightly darker shade of the colour wash and applying it with a very fine watercolour brush. Keep the brush vertical, and let it move slightly as the lines are drawn to vary their thickness. With the small fan brush, blend these lines downwards to replicate the way the rings stretch within the timber. When the painting is complete, seal the treatment with a glaze tinted with yellow ochre to bring out the colours.

Pine
Mix up a more watery colour wash from the colours suggested and apply it in the same way as the oak wash. Then take an old toothbrush and pull it through the wash to create the strong multiple graining that pine has. Pine is a naturally knotty wood and so paint small, egg-shaped knots at 45 degrees to the vertical grain randomly across the board with a darker shade of the colour wash. Lift the centres of the knots out by using a clean, wet brush to make them look more realistic. Leave the result to dry, and then, with a mid-brown water-colour pencil, add the other graining that works with and around the knots. Use a clear PVA glaze to finish the treatment. Apply this vertically with a brush, working down the board so that the glaze pulls some of the coloured pencil lines and blends them into the background.

Walnut
Use a base-coated surface and apply a very thin wash (milk consistency) of Vandyke brown, black and burnt sienna first. Then lift the flashing, as suggested for oak, from top to bottom in a fairly regular, striped pattern. Check this against a reference or an actual piece of timber. Let this dry and then dampen the surface with water and apply a darker

wash of the same colour mix, but slightly thicker and containing a delaying agent. To get the stripe effects, draw a fan brush, from top to bottom, through the wash, to reveal some of the first wash. Then gently blend at right angles to the stripes. To finish, use a walnut-coloured stain and darken the treatment to match the sample or design requirements.

Maple
This type of wood has cloudlike graining that swirls across the timber. Take the prepainted board and dampen it well. Apply a thin colour wash and dab a small artist's sponge into the wash to remove and merge patches of colour. The graining is quite amoeba-like and should be drawn on with a watercolour pencil. For bird's-eye maple, add small, dark brown dots of paint in clusters randomly across the surface to replicate the fungal dots that appear in this timber. This was used extensively in the 1930s for interiors and was always highly polished and a rich honey in colour. Mix oil or acrylic paint into a high gloss varnish to achieve this quality.

Subtle Wood-grain
Where the grain is fine, it is best to use a series of washes to build layers. Use the same procedure and apply a base coat of emulsion paint. Apply the colour in thin washes and, with a dry brush, draw through the wash to reveal the colour underneath. Do this with acrylics so that once one wash has dried it becomes fixed and is not subsequently removed with the next wash. With this method it is important to begin with the lightest washes and build up to the denser colours.

METAL

Copper is one of the few metals with the necessary malleability and versatility for use in scale models. It is readily available in specialist

Exercise: Making a Model 'Rocker'

A rocker is a tool that can be used to add strong grain effects for theatre and interior design purposes. Study a full-size rocker to match the contour patterning on its surface. Take a small piece of foamboard 15mm square and press it into a piece of flattened modelling clay. Then, with the point of a pencil, carefully copy the pattern from the rocker by scoring into the modelling clay. Repeat the process to create several moulds. Then drop in dipping latex from the back end of a brush to carefully fill the moulds, tap the mould to make sure that you release any air bubbles. Allow it to harden off. Select the best cast and, with double-sided adhesive tape, fasten the rocker around the circumference of a round pencil. This is then ready for use.

Creating Bark Effects or Old Timbers Using a Miniature 'Rocker'

Take a piece of ticket card. Study the sample or image of the wood and mix up a base colour that is the same as the background colour of the timber. Paint the card and allow it to dry. Mix up a colour with gouache, water and a delaying agent, in equal parts, to match the graining so that it is of the consistency of cream. Paint an

Using a small-scale rocker to create a heavy, grained, bark effect.

even coating of the mixture over the card. Allow the paint to get to a semi-dry state, then use the rocker to pull through and down the board, allowing the head to rock backwards and forwards in the paint to create the knots and irregular graining. This may need several pulls to create the desired effect. The rocker will need to be cleaned with water quite regularly to avoid its clogging. By experimenting it is possible to achieve different qualities of graining and age.

Right *Sceno-graphic model showing extensive use of stainless-steel metal finishes on the workstations and walls (for* The Kitchen; *designer: Nicholai Hart-Hansen).*

craft stores or by mail order in rod, bar, box and sheet form. When considering any metal surface copper is a good starting point. Use metallic paints to change the copper into any metal surface required. It is relatively inexpensive and solders well. Copper sheeting is available in several gauges down to thousandths of an inch. The finer end of the range is useful for large metal surfaces and can be overlapped and riveted for metal panelling, with small modelling pins in copper or brass.

Another quality of copper is that is can be aged and changed to create interesting finishes by applying a variety of chemicals or heat. When copper ages it naturally turns green with the appearance of verdigris. To create this artificially, apply household ammonia to the surface (follow the instructions regarding use and make sure that the room is well ventilated) with either a brush or by dipping the whole sheet. Leave the treated metal to dry off naturally. To vary or change the amount of verdigris gently rub the surface with wire wool. When copper is heated oxidation occurs and various 'petrol-like', rainbow colours appear. Create this by gently heating the metal with a blowtorch or over a domestic gas-cooker flame. Always wear protective gloves and use plastic-handled pliers to hold the metal sheet since copper is an efficient conductor of heat.

Rusty Metal

To create a rusty finish on metal surfaces there now exist textured, stone-effect pastes, intended for interior design, which produce a texture that, in 1:25 scale, produces a good rust effect. They are available in a rust red colour, but will need further painting to create variance and depth. First, paint the copper or card with metallic enamel paint to the required metal base colour. Apply the product with a brush; it is most effective if the coverage

is patchy. If recreating small patches of rust where water may have run, use the end of a brush and dab small amounts into the recesses. To add runs of rusty water use stripes of acrylic paint to discolour the metal and then paint PVA over it to create the dampness or use oil paint mixed with linseed oil, both will give a good effect.

MARBLING

Like wood-graining, marbling can help to establish a particular historical period and a sense of opulence. As with wood, marble is a natural material used on floors, walls, architectural details and furniture. It is available in numerous varieties and colours. Again, as with wood-graining, it is important to work from good photographic references or samples of actual marble. In a design, marble can be realistic or given a heightened sense of reality, but both need to show the natural qualities of the stone.

There is true depth within marble due to its thickness and how it is cut and polished into slabs or tiles, so the designer or model-maker should work with this information. Look at how marble is formed in layers: it will usually have patterning and veining that is directional. Marble is translucent and has a free-formed, cloudy background and a foreground that reveals its composition through its veining. When considering the use of marble for walls or floors remember that it is cut and supplied as either slabs or tiles and so, realistically, there will need to be joins when covering large areas of the stage. It might be advantageous to design this around the sizes of the timber sheets that will form the set fascias. This will avoid having to match a free-formed patterning across several separate sheets.

Marble looks most effective when taken from a limited palette of earth colours, with the possible additions of Brunswick green, alizarin crimson and cobalt blue. When mixing the colours, always test them against the sample or the photographic image to make sure that the colour washes are true. With marbling it is crucial that the surface being treated is flat and smooth. Use two coats of magnolia emulsion paint on mountboard or foamboard (whichever best suits the particular structure within the model) and lightly sand the first coat before applying the second with a small paint roller.

When painting the background it is important to keep the surface damp so that the paint can naturally move and blend as it is applied. Use translucent paints for this stage to achieve the desired subtlety and depth. Roll the colour on to the wet surface with the side of a watercolour brush. This will avoid your

leaving brush marks in the wash. Once this has dried, the next stage defines the foreground and the type of marble. For these colours use opaque paint, water and a delaying agent to prolong the time available to work with the colour wash.

Veined Marble

Apply the darker colour wash in the same random, flowing fashion, but this time include the direction that the marble contains. Do this without first dampening the surface. Take a piece of tissue paper, scrunch it up and dab it lightly against the surface to remove areas of paint (the technical term for this is frottage). Try other fine papers, fine natural cotton or cling film to give different effects. Before the paint has fully dried, use the small fan brush to

Preparing samples of different types of marble, here using a wet brush to remove parts of the veining to create a more realistic finish (scenic artist: Sue Dunlop).

A designer using a watercolour pencil to replicate the veining on a marble sample (student designer: Michelle Douek).

blend the patterning to remove some of the harshness. Add the veining as an off-white colour with either a very fine brush or a sharp watercolour pencil. Use the brush vertically so that the line moves freely and has a varying thickness. Add variance by applying a damp brush to the veining either to pick out the centres of the lines or to push the paint back on itself to make the lines thinner in places.

Striped Marble

This marble has strong directional graining running in a parallel pattern within its composition. Apply the foreground colour wash, with the addition of a delaying agent, in stripes across the board to match the direction in the marble. Tear a strip off a thin plastic bag and stretch it into a finer strip, forming natural folds. Hold it between thumbs and forefingers and dab it across the surface of the paint, working with the directional wash. If it fills in too much then a wet brush will remove some of the excess. Do further detailing by using artist's pencils.

Stone-chipped Marble

The formation of this marble involves different fragments of stones that have been geologically brought together in a tightly formed conglomerate. Create the background in the same way as with the other marbles. For the foreground, take a small, natural, artist's sponge. Look for one that has a tight and varying surface. Apply the colour washes for the stones direct on to different areas of the sponge. Dampen the surface of the board with a wet brush and gently dab the sponge on the surface, turning it all the time so that a mix of colour is applied across the entire surface. A sense of depth will naturally occur as the surface dries out and the paint applied becomes more pronounced. Add further detail with artist's pencils. Heavy areas of paint may be broken up with water on a fine brush.

Glazing

Once the paint treatments are complete, the surface needs to be glazed. For old or lightly polished marble use a mix of PVA and water. For highly polished marble, use a high gloss varnish.

Uneven Marble Surfaces

Where furniture and architectural features are marble some of these methods will need to be adapted. Begin by applying the base colour of magnolia emulsion; however, it will be difficult to produce wet washes so instead use watercolour pencils to shade the patterning, then with a damp brush blend and merge the shading.

Colour photocopying a finished treatment on to paper of good quality provides large quantities of marbling where large areas of staging need an even colour match. This paper version can be cut and assembled more easily on small scenic elements and furniture, and by rolling and glueing the paper around tubes it is possible to form marble columns and plinths.

PEELING PAINT

To create cracked, pealing paint use a craft crackle glaze, obtainable from DIY stores. This will provide a crackle effect that is suitable for flooring or large surface areas. Change the colour by adding washes or rubbing gouache or acrylic into the surface. However, for doors, windows or furniture, the scale of the crackle effect is too great. A similar effect can be achieved by applying a gouache colour over an enamel-paint undercoat. If the gouache is applied before the enamel has completely dried, then the different media should create the cracking. The surface can also be adjusted by using fine-grade sandpaper to rub down the surface and reveal the second surface colour. If the treatment is applied to a plastic or metal, then small sections can be peeled back by using a scalpel blade.

GLASS

For all the different types of glass begin the process with clear acetate sheeting. The type for use with a personal computer printer is ideal. Use this untreated for modern glass. Be careful when glueing the glass into a frame because the clear adhesive will permanently mark the surface.

Frosted Glass
Use two sheets of the acetate and sandwich clear, double-sided tape between the sheets to give an opaque quality. If the tape is wider than the pane of glass then it will also provide a means of fastening it to the frame.

Etched Glass
Mask out the design on the acetate with either masking tape or artist's masking fluid. Spray the surface with fine, even coats of an etching spray (wear a face mask when doing this). The spray is obtainable from DIY and craft stores. Once the etch has dried, remove the tape or fluid to reveal the transparent design.

Dimpled Glass
Use PVA glue and dab spots of it on to the surface of the acetate with the end of a paint brush. When it has dried it provides the required dimples and opaqueness.

Old Glass
Spray a very fine dusting of yellow ochre enamel paint on to the surface of the acetate. When this has dried, apply liberal amounts of clear adhesive to the surface and allow it to harden completely. This will give the aged, unrefined quality that ancient glass has.

A Victorian front porch, showing the use of stained glass in and above the door (student designer: Sara Svensson).

Stained Glass
There are numerous glass paints on the market for interior design and hobby crafting, but for scenographic models these may be too bright and modern. Lighten by adding turpentine or mix together with each other to create more realistic colours. First apply the leading design, which in a real window holds the coloured glass in place, using contour-lining paste piped directly on to the acetate, following the required design. Once this has hardened, use a fine brush and apply the glass paint to fill in between the leading where it is necessary. If the colour is too light, apply extra coats to darken the colour for the correct colour match.

4 CREATING INTERIORS

Before beginning to make scenographic models for performance it is important for the designer to be armed with enough techniques and knowledge to support his or her personal creativity. There will be times where a more naturalistic approach to interiors is what is required, so the following methods for creating scale interiors will become an important resource. The examples listed in the next three chapters will not cover all eventualities, but, by creatively applying and combining techniques, different periods, architectural details and finishes can easily be achieved.

FLOORING

Flooring is quite often the surface that the audience see most of, particularly if they are in the upper circle of a proscenium theatre or watching theatre-in-the-round. Therefore it should be a designer's first consideration when beginning to develop any design. It provides the foundation for any further staging ideas

Opposite A section of the scenographic model for Present Laughter *at Central School of Speech and Drama*

Painted marble floor designed to fit with 1930s décor, for Present Laughter *(director: Angie Langfield; actors: Tim Steed and Laura Jo McFall).*

and is the surface with which the actors make the most physical contact. The quality of the surface may also be crucial for a lighting designer, depending upon how absorbent or reflective of light the colour, the texture or the finish is.

Floorboards

Different periods of history, or even countries, have or had differently sized floorboards, so that this element needs researching. For example, in the Tudor period, floorboards were shorter and wider than at the present – to ease their removal and transporting since it was normal to take the floor up when moving from house to house.

Consider the layout of the boards in relation to the room: floorboards are usually supplied in set lengths and are arranged in a staggered pattern that fits with the supporting joists. Consideration should also be given to the relationship of the floorboards to the walls and the doors in a room. For example, having floorboards radiating from a main entrance will give that entrance more emphasis within a stage design.

It is useful to draw the floor layout and to mark out the floorboards before assembly. Then, with a prepainted sheet of mountboard (see chapter 3 for wood-graining technique) cut out each individual board. Secure the floorboards to the base of the model by using double-sided tape. Colour the edges of the mountboard with a black marker before assembly so that, when laid, the gaps between the boards appear in shadow. For nail holes, press a compass point into the card. The resulting floor can then be glazed, to represent a polished one, by applying a mixture of equal parts of PVA and water.

Parquet and Heavily Patterned Flooring

Copy or design the floor on to blue graph paper. Then, with a fine 0.1 ink pen, draw in the outlines of the design. Prepare a sheet of cartridge or watercolour paper with either the marbling or wood-graining effect that is required. Place this paper in the print tray of a photocopier, then, by using your graph paper pattern, photocopy the design on to the coloured paper. This can be done for all the colours or materials that make up the floor. For parquet flooring, complete sheets may be spray-mounted direct on to the base of the model. With a multipatterned floor, each coloured section needs to be cut out individually and reassembled in the model.

Tiled Flooring

The same technique can be used to create tiled floors. However, to create a more realistic flooring, cut each individual tile out and mix the tiles up before assembling them, this will use the variance in colour and treatment that occurs across the hand-painted sheet of paper. By turning each consecutive tile 90 degrees, wood- or marble-graining can create a natural chequerboard design.

Linoleum Flooring

For patterned linoleum flooring, scan the design into a drawing package on a computer. Make adjustments where necessary to the colour. Reduce the pattern to the correct scale and then repeat the image to form the floor design. Print this on to an A4 sheet of paper. This can then be cut to shape and glued direct to the base of the model by using a spray adhesive. Photographic or brochure-quality paper will automatically provide the necessary sheen.

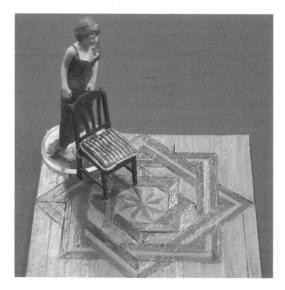

1:25-scale model of a designed parquet wooden floor (student model-maker: Kerry Shepherd).

Scenographic model showing the use of carpet (hand-painted paper) and linoleum (computer-generated) for Sylvia's Wedding, Oldham Coliseum Theatre.

Carpets and Rugs

There are several ways of creating scale carpets. Specialist model shops sell scale rugs and a self-adhesive, backed material for carpeting dolls' houses. The self-adhesive material comes in a range of single colours; to change the colour or create simple patterns, paint into the pile by using acrylics and inks. For more complex carpet designs, take images from reference books or the internet, or design and draw them freehand. Then scan these images into a drawing program on a computer to adjust the colours and reduce the image to the correct scale. Printing on to a coarse watercolour paper will break up the pattern slightly to create an acceptable facsimile of woven wool.

DOORS

Before you decide on the size and the look of the doors used on the set, it is important to analyse their use. Which way will they open: upstage, so that they become self-masking? Or downstage to reveal another space? On-stage or off-stage opening may also have an impact on the type of entrance the actors can make. Are they single or double doors? Double doors upstage centre can provide a grand entrance

where the actor's shape will be framed by the doorway. The opening may also be important for the positioning of lights. The doorway could provide a dramatic statement, with light spilling on-stage into a darkened room setting from either outside or another room.

Secondly, it is important to consider the period. What clothing are the actors wearing? Do they have structured attire that may mean that the doorway has to be widened to accommodate their costume? There may even be tall hats or wigs that will affect the height of the doorframe, or the actors themselves may be physically much larger than average. Sometimes large furniture or props have to be set or struck during the performance, and so it is essential that this information is available before the doors are positioned and made.

Research and produce a line drawing for the selected doors. Ideas concerning period details can be obtained from interior design books, but, wherever possible, visit a house that is of the right period and status. This will provide a much more accurate sense of colour, patina and shape, particularly regarding the width of the walls, and therefore of the doorframes, and of the contours that exist within the panelling.

When modelling the door it is important that you plan for the hingeing mechanism

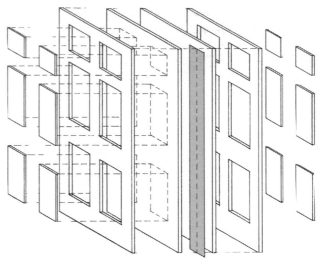

Finished, 1:25-scale doorway from the model of **Educating Rita** *(student model-maker: Kerry Shepherd).*

Diagram showing the assembly of the door and inclusion of fabric hingeing.

first. A thin strip of fine black silk or some other very lightweight fabric gives both durability and flexibility. This strip should be 8mm wide and run the entire length of the door. To provide an invisible means of fastening, the door has to comprise at least two pieces of card sandwiched together with the hinge between them.

Panelled doors are best made with several layers of ticket card glued together to provide the detail and the thickness; in this way the mouldings can be built into the layering. Draw the design for the panelled door on to blue graph paper with a 0.1 ink pen. Then photocopy the design on to several sheets of wood-grained card. Cut and assemble the different layers; remember to glue the hinge into the door before fastening on the first layer. Use double-sided tape to fasten each layer together – this will give clean lines within the mouldings. For painted doors, use plain card and apply emulsion paint after the assembling.

When fastening the door in place, check the way that it needs to open and glue the fabric hinge to the side of the wall that the door opens on to. When making the doorframe, make one side 1mm shorter and 1mm narrower. This will then provide a stop to make sure that the door does not open past its closed position. For the finishing touches cut and glue small strips of gold foil on to the hinged edge of the door to represent brass hinges; use small, painted beads as door knobs; handles can be made from either card or copper wire, depending on the style required; finger plates can be cut out of ticket card and painted to suit.

For glass-panelled doors, use the same methods but substitute clear acetate for the ticket card at the centre of the door.

WINDOWS

There are similar considerations to those suggested for doors to be borne in mind when looking at the purpose of windows within the stage design. How do the actors interact with the windows? Do they have to look out of them? Do they have to open them? Does someone climb through them? These will all have an impact on their size and construction.

The position and the shape of the window might also be determined by lighting opportunities. Windows provide the lighting designer with a golden opportunity to use the frames as a natural gobo, allowing light to stream in and provide a key source for a scene.

Explore and design the window as a 0.1 line drawing on blue graph paper. If the window is to be glazed, then prepare a sheet of acetate following the methods explained in chapter 3. Cut the sheet of acetate to the same dimensions as the entire window, including the frame. Use the line drawing as a template and photocopy the design for the window frame on to ticket card. This could also be done on a computer by scanning in the drawing and printing it out.

For wood or metal window frames, a series of cut-outs from the print-outs can be assembled on top of each other to create the mouldings required by the style of frame and mullions. Paint these before glueing the sheet of acetate to the back. If the window is more sculptural, such as one made of stone, then use mountboard and coat with modelling paste or gesso. Stipple the paste or gesso with a stencil brush as it begins to dry off to create the stone texture and then paint with acrylic or gouache paints.

If the window is to be viewed from both sides, due to its angle on stage or turned around in a scene change, then repeat the process on the other side. Remember that the outside of a window frame will have a different moulding and is narrower to allow for the putty or beading. The finish may also be different on an exterior side because of weather deterioration.

For leaded windows, use a contour-lining paste. This may be purchased from craft shops and is designed for use on glass. The tube will have a fine directional nozzle so pipe the paste straight on to the surface of the acetate. For detailed leading patterns, position the drawing under the acetate, hold in place by using masking tape and then trace over the design with the paste.

If a window has to be opened use the same process as for the hingeing of a door. The width of the fabric may need to be narrower to fit the design and it is best to use a light grey rather

The set for **Educating Rita** *in pre-set light, showing the window being used as a key indicator for the light source (Oldham Coliseum Theatre; lighting designer: Phil Clarke).*

Piping contour-lining paste on to acetate to create the leading for a window, using a photocopy of the design from the technical drawing as a template (student model-maker: Kerry Shepherd).

Staircase with entrances on two levels made from mountboard covered in a self-adhesive felt (for Present Laughter*).*

than a black fabric. Add window catches and latches by using copper wire bent into shape with long nose pliers. Paint these with enamel paint and add on to the finished window.

STAIRCASES

Staircases will form an integral part of any model that has more than one level within the stage design. This is also an aspect of a design that has safety implications. Whether these stairs, or treads, are on- or off-stage they need to be *easily* and *safely* accessible by both actors and stage crew. On-stage stairs should have a handrail as part of the design if they rise more than 2m above the stage. Because of the need to get on- and off-stage quickly, the backstage treads should always have a handrail for anything more than six treads, and the treads themselves should be edged with white tape to make them more visible.

Carefully consider the size of risers and treads. The standard ratio is 3:2, three being the tread and two being the riser. Measurements may be taken from actual stairs to suit, but the standard sizes are 300mm treads and between 200 and 250mm risers. These are natural proportions that actors will feel at ease with. It may be that space does not allow for this ratio or that, as a requirement, the stairs should be difficult to climb. If this is the case, try to test out what this means in actuality before modelling an entire flight that might prove impossible to work with. It is also worth considering what the actors are wearing on their feet: high heels or loose-fitting shoes may make an entrance precipitous useless these are considered in the design and the making of the model.

For a basic, straight set of treads, 1,000-micron mountboard is the best material as it will hold its shape over normal widths of staircase without bowing or needing a central support. Draw up and cut out the side supporting walls first. When drawing up the treads and risers, remember that the thickness of the card on the treads will reduce the depth needed for the risers, so allow for this when marking up and cutting out. The treads can then be assembled by using clear adhesive.

Deal with panelled stair fascias in a similar way to panelling on doors by building up layers of ticket card on top of a mountboard fascia. For modelling the newel post, use small-scale box timber and beads to create the necessary turned shapes. Make the handrail from strips of ticket card of differing width sandwiched together to create the contours. For the spindles, carve and sand down matchsticks, or alternatively, turned spindles can be modelled by using 0.1mm piano wire with tubing and beads threaded on to the wire to create the required contours. To get the angle of the rail and the length of the spindles right, do a line drawing and cut each piece to fit the drawing. With such a mixture of materials, use cyano-acrylate glue to fasten everything together. Once assembled, it is best to give the whole staircase a coat of emulsion paint before applying the particular final paint effect.

For more detailed banisters and panels, such as those of wrought iron, cut the design out of black ticket card. Add dimension to the fretwork by using contour-lining paste. Paint the panels with a pewter enamel paint to get a wrought-iron finish. For gilt work, use the same method and spray the finished panels with a bright, gold spray paint (this can then be neutralized and aged with a light dusting of a matt black spray paint).

Curved or Sweeping Staircases

For staircases that incorporate sweeping curves, draw a plan view of the staircase and use this as a template to cut out the individual treads. It is useful to number them on the reverse side to avoid mixing them up. Cut out the risers to match the height that has been set. With quick-drying, clear adhesive, attach a riser to the underside of each tread. Cut enough small, triangular supports to glue under each tread to make sure that the angle between the tread and the riser is a constant 90 degrees. Begin to assemble the staircase from the ground up. When joining all the sets of risers and treads to each other, glue a support, made of ticket card, to the ends of each new step. These triangular supports should match the length of the tread and the height of the riser. This may have to be measured for each step as the curve changes. The supports will help to keep the staircase in shape during its construction and can be retained or cut away when further structure is added.

If the understairs space is enclosed to the floor, this can be calculated by placing cartridge paper against the staircase and drawing around the shape to create a pattern. The banister has to follow the same curve and angle as the stairs. Create the pattern for this by turning the finished flight of stairs upside down and using the outside edge to draw around. Neaten the curve of the pattern by using a flexi-curve and cut out either one or a series of ticket-card strips, depending on the style and the thickness of the banister rail.

Spiral Staircases

These are made in a similar way to curved staircases, but in this case the plan view drawn for the treads will be a full or partial circle divided into a number of segments, based on the diameter of the circle (the space available) and the width that the treads need to be. The outside edge of each tread should be 300mm wide. Use a protractor and a calculator to work out and mark up the angles to form the segmented circle. If with 200mm risers the staircase does not reach the second level, then add additional segments. Remember to cut a circle out of the middle of the same diameter as the central newel pole before cutting out the individual treads.

Make the newel pole from wooden dowelling or plastic tube. Cut and intersperse with beads to create a more ornate, turned, central pole, if you are following a particular style or period. Use epoxy resin glue to assemble the several elements of the pole since it provides a strong bond. Paint this before attaching the treads to it. For treads that have no risers, cut an angled support that runs under the centre of each tread. This should be tapered towards the outside edge and deep enough at the other one to secure the tread firmly to the newel pole (approximately 15 degrees). Paint the treads before securing them into position. If the staircase has risers, then use the same process as previously described.

Measure the height that the staircase has to reach and then divide that by 200mm; this will give you the number of treads required. Small adjustments may need to be made to ensure that the stairway reaches to the second level accurately. Begin assembling the spiral from the base up. Glue the first step into position with contact adhesive. Because this forms an instant bond, the staircase can be assembled without long delays being incurred while waiting for the previous treads to set. Each tread, when viewed from above, should slightly overlap the one below and be at 90 degrees to the central pole.

To add handrails and calculate the distance between the uprights (they should be centred on the outside edge of each or selected treads), create a tube, made from a piece of tracing paper, around the outside of the staircase and, with a pencil, mark the centre and draw the edge of each tread. Open up the sheet of paper, join the points and measure this angle with a protractor. On a piece of graph paper, plot and draw this angled line projected from one of the

Above *Attaching the first treads to the newel post to create a spiral staircase (student model-maker: Kerry Shepherd).*

The finished spiral staircase (student model-maker: Kerry Shepherd).

horizontal lines on the paper. Use this line as the handrail. Now draw in the lengths and positions of the uprights, using the tracing as a reference. Cut two strips of ticket card to correspond with the length and the depth of the handrail. Position one of the strips for the handrail along the angled line. Position and glue the uprights to this by using clear adhesive, then glue the second handrail strip over that.

To help to create a smooth curve, first paint the inside of the handrail. When this is dry, gently curve the handrail by winding it around a toilet roll. Tack it at both ends to the roll with masking tape. Paint the outside of the staircase while it is positioned around the toilet roll. As the paint dries, it will help the staircase to keep its shape. Slide it off the toilet roll and glue into position on the outside edge of the staircase. Small, vertical, interior supports may need to be added to the uprights to keep the rail vertical as it winds around the staircase.

Use open-weave embroidery canvas to create open-mesh stairs and fire escapes. When sprayed with a mixture of matt black and metallic paint, it provides a good surface that can be cut to shape with scissors but is robust and light enough to support itself. Frame the edge of each tread with fine strips of ticket card.

WALLCOVERINGS

Wallpaper

The choice of modelling method will depend on how the finished wallcovering is to appear on stage. If the scenic artists are going to create the pattern by screen printing or stencilling a design, then the model will be a better match if it is executed freehand. Paint a base colour on wall with emulsion paint, and then with a fine brush, or a cut stencil in the case of a large pattern, paint or stencil the design direct on to the wall.

Wallpaper created by scanning a design, then reducing and repeating the pattern in a computer design program (student designer: Jane Barker).

Where the walls of the set are going to carry actual wallpaper, it is best to print up a miniature version of it and paste this on to the model. Take the design from a reference book or image and scan it into a computer to make adjustments to the colour and size. The pattern can then be repeated to create scale strips one-and-a-half times the length of the wall in the model, and 550mm wide in 1:25 scale (the extra length is to allow for matching the pattern). Print these out on to the thinnest quality paper that will feed through the colour printer. Apply the finished scale wallpaper strips on to the wall by using double-sided tape to get a completely flat finish. Alternatively, you could draw out the whole wall within the computer program and assemble and print the complete section in one step.

Wood panelling made by the cut-card method, but with thin strips of wire to create beading around the panels (designer: Simon Kenny).

Creating wallpaper in strips makes the representing of ageing and peeling of sections simpler. For mould, dab turpentine on so that it soaks into the paper and then add fine dots of oil paint to create the mould effect. Where torn wallpaper is required, use PVA instead of double-sided tape to fasten the strips up. Once this has dried out, tear the paper away to fit the required level of distress. If the wallpaper needs to appear as if it had peeled away naturally from the wall, glue with PVA the fastened section to the wall, then paint the back of the hanging paper with a yellow ochre wash and, while it is still wet, curl it into the selected position. Remember to paint the plastered wall where it is going to be exposed before glueing on the wallpaper.

Wood Panelling

Draw out the wall with all its panels, skirting board, dado rail and picture rail with a 0.1 black ink pen on to blue graph paper. Create the wood graining and type of timber as a paint treatment on to sheets of A4 that will feed through a photocopier. Run off the number of copies that represent the number of sheets required to create the depth of moulding within the panels. Take the first sheet and, with a scalpel, cut out all the panels to the first line of the moulding, making sure that the cut completely removes the black line. With spray adhesive, fasten this sheet to a sheet of prepainted surface that has not been through the photocopier. Repeat the overlay with a second sheet from which the panels have been cut away to the next moulding line. Continue this process until you have completed all the levels. Further painting and glazing may be done once the wall has been assembled.

SKIRTING BOARDS, DADO RAILS, PICTURE RAILS, ARCHITRAVES AND CORNICES

Layers of ticket card cut into strips and fastened together with double-sided tape can create the profiles in these architectural mouldings. Use varying thicknesses of card to create a more accurate copy of the contours. Paint the ticket-card moulding with emulsion paint which will soften the hard cut edges and corners to better replicate the curves in the profile of the mouldings. When fastening these to the walls of a set, mitre the corners of thicker mouldings to create an accurate fit into and around corners. Purchase or make small mitre blocks to help achieve this. When fastening an architrave around a door, cut the ends to 45 degrees to create right-angled corners where vertical and horizontal lengths meet.

Specialist model stores sell mouldings for dolls' houses that, although not in 1:25 scale, may be cut down and sections of them used for mouldings and the architrave. A combination of card and bought mouldings will help to create the deeper details such as ornamental cornices.

ARCHES, COLUMNS AND PILASTERS

When creating arches, it is always important to get the thickness of the walls right. This will vary considerably between historic periods and with the status of the property's owner. Good references or actual measurements from period houses are essential in getting these features correct. Use 1,000-micron mount-board to form the basic arch; this should be

Model showing the use of a mixture of cut card and bought mouldings to create the skirting boards, dado and cornice on an arts and crafts period room (designer: Rose Clarke).

Exercise: Creating Small-scale Plaster Mouldings

As an alternative, make real plaster mouldings using a scaled-down technique employed by manufacturers of mouldings and ceiling roses called 'sledging'. Take a piece of 0.5mm plastic (50mm × 50mm), cut a profile of the moulding that you wish to create along the bottom edge of this plastic. Attach a strip of box balsa wood to the top edge to use as a strengthener and handhold. Take an A3 piece of Perspex and screw a piece of 1in × 1in timber to it to act as a runner for the profile. Mix up modelling plaster as directed on the package and, when it is ready, channel a strip down the length of the Perspex. Push the profile up against the runner and pass the profile through the plaster in both directions. Clean the profile as necessary and repeat the passing action until a perfect strip of moulding appears. Keep going until it has completely hardened and it will yield a polished and perfectly formed strip of plaster moulding. When it is finished, carefully prise it off the Perspex, then cut and assemble it as required.

Photograph showing the profile and finished piece of moulding prepared by using the technique described (method and model devised by Tony Banfield).

This works best with heavier mouldings such as those around proscenium arches. Dado rails and architraves are too fine and the plaster will crumble.

flexible enough to bend to form most curves without buckling or cracking. With small arches use two sheets of ticket card glued together. To create the mouldings around arches, use ticket card cut into radial sections that, when mounted together, create the required contours. More elaborations, such as keystones, pediments, pilasters and period embellishments, may be added at this stage, by a combination of ticket card, modelling putty and contour-lining paste. To create an even plaster finish, paint over the finished archway with emulsion paint or gesso.

Create simple vertical columns by rolling cartridge paper around a piece of dowelling that has a slightly smaller diameter than the required finished column. Cut a strip of cartridge or watercolour paper (already painted to match the required construction material) that is the equivalent of the height of the column and 210mm in length. Lay it face down on a flat surface and fasten a piece of double-sided tape at one end of the strip. At the other end, place the dowel on the edge and begin to roll the paper around it, making sure that it keeps in line. Roll right to the end and the double-sided tape will fasten it all together. Slide the finished column off the dowel. The paint effect will need only minor adjustments to cover up the join.

For tapering columns, begin with a dowel and build air-drying, modelling putty to get the correct profile. The finished surface can be refined by using fine-grade sandpaper once the putty has completely hardened. Where columns need to be fluted, use the edge of a steel rule and press it into the modelling putty while it is still wet to create the vertical ridging.

Card circles and buttons glued together will provide capitals and bases. For more detailed periodic capitals, such as the Ionic or the Corinthian, use oven-firing modelling putty to model most of the structure and details. Once fired, add final, intricate embellishments with contour-lining paste. Once the capitals and bases are assembled, they should be given a coat of emulsion or gesso, depending upon on the texture being replicated. Use marbling, wood-graining, gilding or stone effects to complete the process.

FIREPLACES

Since the fascias of fireplaces are made up of columns, arches and plinths, use scaled-down versions of previously discussed modelling techniques. Make the internal structure for the chimney breast with black mountboard stippled with black emulsion. Further colours may be added to vary the smoke staining by using gouache or acrylics. Make the hearth, if it is a solid piece of stone or marble, from mountboard and paint it accordingly. If the fireplace contains tiling, use coloured ticket card or scan and print out photographic images for detailed patterned tiles. Cut these out as individual tiles and assemble them on to the surround. Make grates from black ticket card with contour-lining paste piped on to the

Modelling an ornate archway with pediment and supporting Corinthian columns, all made from modelling putty and several thicknesses of card.

1:25 scale model of a Victorian fireplace showing the white-card construction with added contour-lining paste detail, finished with wood-graining by using acrylics.

An ornate plaster ceiling under construction from foamboard, ticket card, modelling putty and contour-lining paste.

surface to give structure to the bars and create the contours that exist in cast-iron grates. To finish, dust with a faint spray of metallic paint. Make coal from cork chippings glued into the required block and then spray painted matt black.

CEILINGS

Ceilings are one aspect of interiors that rarely appear on stage because the lighting rig takes up that position. However, there are some occasions where, with partial ceilings or exaggerated perspectives, they can become a design feature.

For plaster-moulded ceilings, use the same technique as has already been suggested for wood panelling, but in this case photocopy the pattern on to white ticket card and assemble in the same way. Extra details may be piped on with contour-lining paste, or, for large-scale ornamentation, sculpted from oven-firing modelling putty and glued into position .The whole surface can be completed with a coat of white or cream emulsion paint or gesso.

Build ceiling roses by using layers of card circles or rings. For the ornamentation within the rose, cut patterns from old lace or paper doilies and combine these with the cut card. A coat of cream or white emulsion paint will cover any differences in material and produce a plaster finish. For highly decorated roses, use modelling putty and contour-lining paste to form the intricate designs. Tongue-and-groove panelled ceilings may be made by following the same procedure as with floorboards.

To create oak beams, use mountboard to create the basic framework or struts. Generously apply modelling paste or gesso to the card surface, allowing a rough texture to form. Knots and additional graining can be added by drawing a pin through the paste while it is wet. Whittle matchsticks down to a diameter of 1.5mm, cut 1mm slices off the sticks and glue to the beams to represent the location pegs. Paint the wood effect required by using gouache, acrylic or specialist scenic paints. Then give the whole framework a light dusting with a matt black spray paint to age it and make it appear more rustic.

5   CREATING EXTERIORS

INTRODUCTION

The most difficult type of environment to create effectively on stage is an exterior location. The audience recognizes artificiality immediately. Therefore the designer's role is to understand this and use the resources available to play with the illusion.

Lighting and sound can have a profound effect on creating illusion. It is important, when deciding on materials, colours and textures, that there is some experimentation with samples and possible lighting effects. Even real grass used on stage can look completely artificial if lit incorrectly. When modelling, test out the samples by using a focusing torch and lighting gels to see how coloured light changes the qualities of the model environment. As a designer/model-maker it is impossible to make demands concerning lighting states, but it is always important to know how surfaces will react.

Sound can also enhance the illusion, from the twittering of birds or the noise of traffic to a full orchestral score. What makes the illusion more real is sound surrounding the stage so that the audience hears both dimension and

Opposite *The front door and outside wall that was a section of the stage set for* Sylvia's Wedding *at Oldham Coliseum.*

focus. This may necessitate the need to build speakers into the design itself, but they are now so compact that it is easy to hide them in shrubs or other scenic elements that will not block the sound. Where this is not possible and speakers need to be built into solid structures, the openings these create can be covered by scenic gauze and painted to blend with the rest of the set. It is not necessary to include these in the model but locations need to be considered.

Exteriors also give the designer a good opportunity to surprise the audience with such things as smoking chimneys, working fountains or running water and breezes that waft the actor's hair and clothing. It is now even possible to inject smells into a theatre space to help to create an atmosphere.

These 'tricks' incorporated into the design and the finished scenographic model will help to develop a sense of place that can provoke or engage an audience to respond to a particular space when it is used in performance.

SKIES AND PANORAMAS

In reproducing exterior locations, one of the most important indicators of mood or atmosphere is the sky; as in everyday life, the way we approach our day is greatly influenced by the weather. The sky can be a visual barometer, conveying conditions that we tend

Scenographic model showing the use of a lit cyclorama and cut-out trees to create the extensive grounds of a Russian dacha in **Summerfolk** *(student designer: Margaret Harrris).*

Production shot from **Summerfolk** *showing how the lighting has created depth and heightened realism on the trees (student lighting designer: Michelle Walsh; actress: Ellie O'Keeffe).* Photo: Amy Bunyard

to read in a certain way or mood. So in a theatre, where there is little opportunity to change the temperature, a well designed and painted sky can evoke the blustery conditions of the windswept heath for *King Lear* or the lazy sunny days of *Much Ado About Nothing.*

The simplest form of sky-cloth is the white cyclorama that, through single or multiple use of coloured lighting states, can provide an impression of a sky and the variance of colour that occurs at different times of day. This type of sky is more often used when the staging is more abstract or where the sky plays a less dominant role. Where the sky becomes, in effect, another actor, then there will be a need for a more detailed and specific sky. Here, a

painted cyclorama or cloud projection (moving clouds) or a combination of these can achieve this.

A sky backdrop in the model can be as simple as a sheet of coloured card or a photocopied/scanned image suspended at the back of the model. Where the cyclorama needs to wrap around the stage, a frame made from foamboard will both stretch and maintain the curve. In some instances, lighting cycloramas from behind can be effective. Photocopying or printing on to tracing paper can provide the necessary translucency to enable the cyclorama to be backlit in the model. The image of the sky can also carry over on to the stage legs and borders to create a complete wraparound picture within the proscenium, but with the advantage of multiple entrances; create this by using several copies of the sky image and spray glueing it in sequence across the legs and borders.

One of main reasons for using a painted cloth is to allow the designer the opportunity to make the sky relevant to a particular performance. A heavy, brooding sky will create a sense of doom or impeding disaster, or clouds painted in perspective can create both a sense of movement and of depth. The angle of the clouds can also create a focus to a particular area of the stage that may have especial significance.

In these instances, the designer/model-maker will have to create his or her own designs. The use of extremely wet washes of colour on watercolour paper or coloured mountboard can be a quick and immediate method of creating a sky-cloth for the model. Let the bleeding and merging that naturally and accidentally occur help to create the right atmosphere: use large, sable-haired brushes and keep the movement fluid to avoid the creation of edges. Always consider the direction of the sun when painting skies. How does it catch the top or the bottom of the clouds? Use masking fluid during the colour washes to retain those bright areas where the sun is bursting through heavy, clouded skies. Add the sun's rays by shading over the painted clouds with coloured pencils. Airbrushing is a useful technique to master when painting skies for models. This closely matches the spray-gun technique used by the scenic artist when creating numerous staging effects, including skies.

Production shot showing how the design and painting of a sky cloth can draw emphasis to a certain aspect of the staging, in this instance, the model house (The Secret Rapture; *director: Angie Langfield; actress: Sarah Guyler*).

Painting the sky cloth for a model by adding the light to the tops of the clouds.

Exercise: Lighting Up the sky

In the planning and designing of a sky-cloth the choice of colours is crucial. Colours react differently under different lighting states. Some will almost disappear or become more dominant depending on the light that illuminates them. This may be due to the tone, hue or the amount of UV that is present in the colour.

To test this out, make up a sample board of all the colours as separate blocks on an A4 sheet of white mountboard. Take a focusable torch and a swatch book of sample lighting gels (available from manufacturers and specialist model stores) and, in a darkened room, test each colour with a variety of coloured gels by shining the light through the colour. Make notes on how the colour reacts. Keep the samples and results on file so that they become a useful resource for discussions with the lighting designers on future projects.

Night Skies

The theatrical product most often used when recreating a night sky is a star-cloth. This black, serge cloth has LEDs or fibre optics sewn into it to create the stars. For model-making purposes, use a sheet of black mountboard and, with a silver glitter glue pen, place dots from the pen to represent the constellations. Varying the size of the dots creates the illusion of distance. When the model is then lit, the specks of glitter will catch the light and shimmer like a star-cloth.

Sky Gauzes

Painted shark's-tooth gauzes can be used to build up depth within a sky. When designs for skies are painted on to this material and placed in front of a star-cloth, it becomes possible to transform a scene from day to night. By cross-fading the light from the front of the gauze to the star-cloth, stars will begin to appear as the clouds become less visible. This duality will also provide the flexibility to have a cloudy, starlit night sky.

Sky gauzes, in conjunction with a cyclorama, can surround an actor or an object with the sky or the weather. If the actor or the object is positioned between the gauze and the cyclorama he or it can be isolated with light to suggest suspension in the air. With the addition of a cloud projector a sense of flying can be achieved.

To create gauzes for a model, use fine muslins or silk organza. It is worth testing the material for its translucency with paint before proceeding with the final design. Fasten and stretch the gauze by attaching it to a frame.

The use of a black mountboard as a star-cloth flecked with dots of glitter, which shimmer in the reflected light (The Cosmonaut's Last Message to the Woman He Loved in the Former Soviet Union).

Clamp this frame to the worktop so that the gauze can be airbrushed vertically, then the superfluous paint will blow through the material rather than clogging the holes. Brush stronger lines and colour gently across the top of the weave with gouache paint. The finished model gauze will light in a similar way to the real thing, making possible experimentation with the model before finalising the lighting design and plotting session.

PANORAMAS

Whether seen through an on-stage window or stretching around the back of the stage, a panoramic backcloth can extend the illusion of depth beyond what is physically possible with the on-stage space. By using perspective, a painted cloth can either extend the on-stage details or create a sense of place beyond the main acting area. Refer to 'Perspective Drawing' in chapter 13 of *Stage Design – A Practical Guide* by Gary Thorne for more details (see the Bibliography).

In designing and planning a panorama it is important to consider how much detail you want to include and how the horizon line and layout fits with the on-stage setting. Another important factor to consider is how close the actors will get to it. Any carefully drawn illusion will be broken if the actor's shadow is cast across the cloth or he stands next to an item such as a doorway that has been drawn in false perspective. Begin with simple line sketches to position vanishing points, horizon lines and focal points, then gradually add in more detail and quick washes of colour to establish foreground and background. Once this is working with the stage setting, then the final drawing and painting can begin. With any backcloth the most difficult line is the join between the stage floor and the vertical cloth. Because these planes are at 90 degrees to each other, even the use of the same colour

*The combined use of a painted sky-cloth and sky-gauze can create a strong sense of depth when used together (*The Cosmonaut's Last Message to the Woman He Loved in the Former Soviet Union; *director: Geoff Coleman; lighting designer: Lucy Carter; actors: Dominic Gerrard and Richard Lynwood).*

will appear different. Avoid paths or roads that lead direct from the stage floor on to the backcloth.

Try to incorporate a ground row as it will visually help this jump from three to two dimensions. These can be simple cut-outs or more dimensional. Ground rows can develop into small rakes that merge into the stage floor. The ground row, when positioned at least 1m away from the cloth and 500mm high, can provide a hidden location for stage lighting to illuminate the bottom half of a cyclorama or backcloth. The ground row can become an

Using a cut-out ground row can add location as well as provide a means of hiding the lights for the cyclorama (Strippers; director: Carole Todd; actors: William Maxwell and Nicholas Moss; lighting designer: Mark Howarth; Oldham Coliseum Theatre).

on-stage horizon line. For the model, make these from mountboard or a combination of materials depending on what the ground row is representing. Remember, the scale of any texture will need to be reduced to maintain a sense of distance.

ROOFS AND CHIMNEYS

Slate and Tiled Roofs

Begin the process by making the pitch or pitches of the roof from mountboard. Paint a whole sheet of A4-sized ticket card to resemble the chosen roofing material. Cut the card into strips that are A4 in length and the depth of the tiles. Draw a horizontal pencil line 2mm down from the top of one of the longer edges. Then mark out the widths of the tiles along the full length of the strip. Following the vertical pencil lines, make cuts with a craft knife between each of the tiles as far as the horizontal pencil line. The wider blade of the

craft knife will cut gaps of the right scale between the tiles. Take a strip of double-sided tape cut to the full depth of the tiles and fasten this along the back of the strip over the cut lines. Then continue cutting all the vertical gaps between the tiles. This will give you a strip of tiles held together by the tape. Peel off the backing paper and fasten the tiles on to the pitched roof, beginning at the base and working up the roof. Remember to follow the pattern and the overlap of the roof tiles. The last row of tiles may need to be trimmed to fit. Alternatively, on small sections of roofing each tile can be glued individually to the mountboard with wood adhesive.

Make ridge tiles from the same ticket card cut into individual tiles, scored and folded down the centre to create the angle to match the pitch of the roof, then glue into position. For semi-circular ridge tiles use the same process and then apply air-drying modelling putty over the tiles and shape to suit. Score the mortar lines in with the back of the scalpel blade.

Thatched Roofs

Begin modelling this type of roof with a mountboard structure that includes all the angles and overhangs. The first stage of adding the texture is to create the contours by sculpting air-drying modelling putty over the entire surface of the mountboard. Smooth this out with wet fingers. To get the effect of the reeds, draw a metal Afro comb through the putty, making sure that the pattern and the direction are constant. Keep repeating this action but slightly changing the position of the comb to create the fine detail of the reeds. To sculpt the ends of the roof, where the reeds appear cut, repeatedly stab the comb into the putty. Where there are different levels of thatch, begin with the lowest and work outwards. Then paint the thatch to suit its apparent age. For the stitching and netting that are present on some thatched roofs, use a black hairnet and edge it with black contour-lining paste. A light dusting of dark brown spray paint will soften the paint treatment and add to the overall finish.

Chimney Stacks

Build the brickwork stacks up by using mountboard to create the basic shape. For the brickwork, use one of the techniques discussed in chapter 3. For the chimney pots, use either plastic tubing, beads or the paper roll method used for columns in chapter 4 or modelling putty. The choice of method will depend on the shape and the ornamentation required by the particular historic period. Glue these on to a base plinth made from layers of mountboard and ticket card. Once painted up, glue the pots and the plinth to the stack. It is important to model the chimneys before attending to the rest of the roof since the tiling, flashing and ridge tiles need to be cut around the chimney.

MAKING SMOKE

To create smoke and mist, take a piece of costume wadding and pull it apart with the fingers to get a single layer. Pull and stretch this further to create varying densities. Once sprayed into, with enamel spray paints, it provides an uncanny resemblance of drifting smoke and mist. Small pieces will create smoking chimney pots or smoke in fire grates. Large sections of stretched wadding at floor level will replicate low-level smoke or dry ice.

WINDOWS

Most structure and modelling techniques for windows appear in chapter 4; the additional aspects to be considered are window surrounds, sills and visibility.

Window surrounds may be completely different in style from the rest of the exterior wall, with brick arches and detailing elements. If so, make these surrounds before dressing the rest of the wall. Some may be as elaborate and detailed as a door entrance; here, use techniques already mentioned to suit the style and the period. For a stucco finish, paint with a white emulsion or gesso, for gloss paint use a colour match emulsion and a glaze of PVA. If it is rough stone an

Assembling the tiles on a slate roof (student model maker: Kerry Shepherd).

Putting the finishing touches to a thatched roof by adding the smoke to the chimney (student model-maker: Kerry Shepherd).

application of epoxy car filler sanded and coloured will yield a suitable effect.

When viewing windows from the outside during daylight the room seen through them will appear dark. Attach sections of fine black organza to the reverse of the window frame. This will appear opaque when the model is lit from outside, but, if the room itself is lit, then shadowy objects will become visible.

Exercise: Making a Grand Entrance

Having to make a front door with a porch or portico is an interesting way of using a series of modelling techniques in a single exercise. To consolidate the techniques already explained, model a 1:25-scale door and portico. Find a local one to use as a reference: visit, measure and photograph the doorway. Methods for modelling all these features are contained in this or the previous chapter.

Creating the portico for a Regency House (student designer: Louise Watson).

The front door could be panelled and aged with some peeling paintwork or a highly polished finish. If the door is ancient and wooden, it will have heavily grained timbers and contain studding and heavy iron hinges. For studs and hingeing use black contour-lining paste, then rust or age with acrylics once the paste has hardened. Above the door might be a fanlight or a rectangular window. In some porches glass panels run down one or both sides of a front door. The glass used could be plain, etched or coloured. Porches can vary in style and embellishment. For example, some Victorian porches have ornate tiles set in panels decorating the inside walls, with doorways dressed by columns, capitals and ornate pediments or arches. The floor of the porch might be marble or black with white chequerboard tiling. In the Georgian and the Regency period, doorways and porticos frequently followed classical forms of architecture, with heavy, columned, temple-like entrance ways, either square or semi-circular. Stucco plaster columns often supported the roof or the pediment. However, marble and stone were also popular. Contained within or attached to the doorway of Georgian or Regency townhouses were ornate ironwork railings.

The door may have a letterbox and a doorknocker. Make the letterbox flap from ticket card and add detail by using contour-lining paste. Model the knocker from a combination of 0.6mm copper wire, modelling putty and contour-lining paste.

IVY AND WALL-COVERING PLANTS

To create creeping or climbing plants model the vegetation direct on to the fully textured wall. With a 2B pencil, lightly draw out the branching that will carry the leaves or flower heads. Pipe a brown contour-lining paste on to the wall, following the pencil drawing. Using the oven-firing modelling putty, create the clumps of leaves and flower heads, fire them and glue them on to the branching. Acrylic paint will add shadow and detail. Where there is heavier branching, use dried grape stalks trimmed and glued into position with clear adhesive. Hide the joins with extra foliage. For a self-standing variety, make the branching with 1mm copper wire, either twisted or soldered together. This can then be coated in modelling paste to create a neutral surface for painting texture and colour on to the branches. Add leaves in the same way.

BALCONIES AND BALUSTRADES

Make these architectural details separately and attach them once the rest of the exterior wall has been finished. Good reference sources will help in the planning and building of balconies. It must be decided, before modelling, how many people will stand on the balcony at one time. This is so that the space to be allocated will be big enough for the action necessitated by the text or the director and that there are sufficient supports underneath it to take their weight.

Produce technical drawings, then a simple, white-card assembly to check the proportions of the balusters and the heights of rails before modelling them in three dimensions. Balusters assembled on rods of 0.5mm piano wire will allow the modelling of separate sections of the baluster. A combination of beads and sculptured modelling putty, once threaded on

Above *Adding ivy to the exterior wall and window surround using modelling putty which is then painted with acrylics (student model-maker: Kerry Shepherd).*

Balustrade made from foamboard, ticket card, piano wire and beads (student model-maker: Kerry Shepherd).

Clapboarding used to create the illusion of the house attached to the hairdressing salon (Steel Magnolias; Crescent Theatre, Birmingham).

to the wire, can create the correct profiles. Leave 3mm of wire protruding from each end to locate the baluster into foamboard or balsa wood rails and bases. This will create either a balustrade for a patio or one side of a balcony wall. Finish by stippling with gesso to provide an even base coat for a painted stone effect, or paint in white emulsion to replicate a stucco effect.

If the balcony supports required are to be imposts or structural pilasters then model these from mountboard and ticket card, with additional architectural details made from modelling putty and glued into position with clear adhesive. For fine detail line-work use contour-lining paste. Some balconies will need columns to support their size or weight; make these in the same way as was discussed in chapter 4.

CLAPBOARDING

Certain houses use clapboarding (overlapping, horizontal planks of timber) to either partly or completely cover the outside of buildings. This is particularly prevalent in countries with a natural abundance of timber.

For model making, cut up 1,000-micron, white mountboard into strips that are the length of the wall to be covered and 150mm wide in 1:25 scale. Fasten double-sided tape to the back of each strip. Cut a piece of black mountboard to the size of the wall. If there are windows or doors, cut these sections out before locating the planking. Begin at the base by fastening one strip of clapboarding flat at the bottom of the wall. With the next strip, overlap the first one by 2mm. Repeat this process up the entire wall. Pencil lines drawn in as a guide will make sure that the boards remain parallel.

On houses, vertical planking on the corners neatens and protects the clapboarding. Recreate this by fastening two strips of mountboard 5mm wide running up the entire height of the wall where a corner occurs, one overlapping the other to create a clean edge.

TREES

To have a full-scale tree on stage is to make a bold design statement. It is likely that such a tree will have a character that is important to the concept or to the play itself. The tree in *Waiting for Godot* by Samuel Beckett is an example of this: desolate and isolated, it manages to sprout a single leaf in Act 2, or the tree that is chopped down by the father in *All My Sons by Arthur Miller*, carries a symbolism that goes beyond stage dressing. Although model trees can be purchased they are unlikely to contain the necessary personality or suitability.

Begin by making detailed sketches of the tree. These will be essential when working out the height and the coverage of the branches. Photocopy on to acetate to experiment with its size within the model box. Stand figures with it, is the scale right? Is it blocking important areas of the stage? These sketches may also be invaluable to the constructors when realizing the design.

Work out how much 0.5mm copper wire will be necessary to trace the longest branch from the root to the tip. Count the number of wires that will be required to tackle all the important branches. Some of the small offshoots can be added later, but include as many of the small branches as is possible. Cut equal lengths of copper wire and bundle them together. Bind a piece of masking tape around the bundle where the base of the trunk begins, allowing the wires below to be free to form the roots. Work up the tree, dividing the wires up to form the main branches and taping as each new branch forms. Keep checking the shape with your acetate as you build. Not all the branches will be of the same length; cut back with wire cutters where necessary. The final twigs should be formed from a single strand of wire. Solder extra twigs on to the branches where necessary.

Analyse how much extra girth needs to be added to this wire skeleton: if the tree is, for example, an oak, you will need to sculpt modelling putty on to the trunk and branches to bulk out the framework. If it is a silver birch or an immature tree, then the frame may be full enough already. The finishing texture will also depend on the type of tree. If it has a smooth bark, then apply small strips of tissue paper with PVA adhesive over the whole tree. Coarse barks will need modelling paste applied

and combed to provide the necessary texture. Paint other surface details with acrylics once the texture has dried.

If the tree needs foliage, specialist model shops sell green, open-weave mesh for this purpose (the type with flock already embedded in it). Another option would be to purchase a synthetic sponge with the qualities of real sponge. Pull the sponge apart to create small pieces and paint them with acrylics to assemble on to the twigs as clumps of leaves.

Conifers
Bottle-brushes make effective conifers. Cut the brush to the right length, taper the bristles from their full width at the base to a point at the top. This will give the right profile. Spray paint the whole brush with mid-brown enamel paint. Then, beginning at the base of the tree, coat the bristles in PVA adhesive and sprinkle a dark green flock on to the surface;

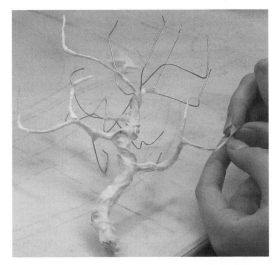

Applying small strips of tissue paper to cover the initial wire frame which gives structure to the branches of a tree (student model-maker: Helen Dufty).

shake off any excess and continue up the tree until it is complete. Alternatively, tear off small pieces of open-weave mesh and push these into the bristles to create an effective layered foliage.

For an inexpensive alternative to flock, collect fine sawdust. Prepare a cold-water dye,

The modelling of a conifer by using a bottle brush as the basic structure.

Formal setting for Vauxhall Gardens, assembled on stage by dropping the false conifers into the crates used throughout the design and adding an ornate working fountain (The Grace of Mary Traverse).

put the sawdust in a stainless container and add just enough dye to colour all the sawdust, spread the sawdust out thinly on to a plastic sheet and allow it to dry.

Hedges

Specialist model stores sell scale box hedging, or, alternatively, expanded open-weave black foam and leaf-green flock for making hedges that contain topiary clipped shapes. For an old or badly cut hedge, pluck out bits of the foam to get the desired shape. Paint PVA on the outside of the foam and dip it into the flock to create the greenery. For the trunks, save the stalks from bunches of grapes; these can dried, trimmed down and glued into position

FORMAL PLANTING

Model stores sell small-scale terracotta pots for creating tubs and pots on patios. Use modelling putty to add extra detail. For finishes other than terracotta, paint the pots with enamel paints to replicate glazes. For unusually shaped pots, model in oven-firing putty around a piece of dowelling for support. Slide them off, fire in the oven and then paint up as required.

Small paper balls from craft shops are excellent for bay trees and topiary. Paint them dark green and add the foliage by applying PVA glue to the surface and rolling the ball around in leaf-green flock. Alternatively, scrunch green tissue paper with more PVA and apply it to the surface, then work with a scalpel point to create a ragged leaf effect. Model other forms by carving the basic shape out of open-weave foam and then create the leaf effect in a similar fashion. For the trunks, use 1mm copper wire with thin strips of tissue wrapped around it and glued to create the right thickness and texture. If the tissue is well soaked in glue it can be manipulated to create interesting offshoots or stumps. Leave 5mm of exposed wire at the top of the trunk to push into the topiary vegetation. The finished shrub can then set into a pot by using air-drying modelling putty. The soil surface can be either painted or have model shingle added in.

Formal gardens such as those attached to grand Tudor houses used box hedging to create the boundaries for intricate patterning, then, by close and careful planting, they created blocks of different colours. Research into the patterns and the plants used will help to make the designs authentic. Craft stores sell packs of vegetation that resemble lichen. These are available in different colours, but a basic green will spray paint to any colour. Add flecks of tissue to create flower-heads.

Fountains

Begin with a length of 1mm piano wire cut to the required height. Around this tape from four to eight lengths of 3 amp fuse wire of double the length of the piano wire, so that the fuse wires are level and extend beyond the piano wire. Then sculpt the shape and details around this central core. Make the base with mountboard and ticket card dressed as stone or marble to suit. Any bowls or statuettes are best modelled from modelling putty and threaded on to or built around the wire core. Once the structure of the fountain is complete and painted, bend the fuse wire down to create spurting water. Cut it to appropriate lengths. Add water to any bowls or reservoirs by filling them with clear adhesive. Trickle clear adhesive over the fuse wire and let it run down to replicate running water.

GRASS

Lawns

Specialist craft stores sell a paper-backed felt that is precoloured for this purpose, which, for a well-kept lawn, provides a quick and accurate facsimile. For lawns that are more formal and need to display the stripes left by

A newly mown lawn made by using the method described.

fresh mowing, use this product and adapt it in the following way: lightly spray with starch half of the felt required to make the lawn and press it with a medium hot iron, then take both the untreated and the ironed felt and cut into 20mm-width strips. Assemble the strips on to the surface required, using alternating strips of untreated and ironed material. With the difference between the piles, an illusion of a newly mown lawn is created.

For long grass, find an old, soft-bristle, household brush. Use enamel spray paints to colour the bristles and then trim off the amount you require. These can then be set into modelling putty to create the required effect.

DRYSTONE WALLING

As drystone walling is made from carefully selected stones stacked horizontally, the modelling of them needs to follow a similar construction. This is time-consuming but well worth the effort. Take a piece of black mountboard cut to the shape required. Take a small piece of modelling putty (the epoxy variety) and roll it out until it is approximately 3mm thick; it is good if the thickness varies,

This dry-stone wall divided the audience from the stage and ran along the side of the seating rostra. It utilized the method described and added frozen snow, with a mixture of icing sugar and clear adhesive (An Experiment with an Air Pump).

FENCING AND RAILINGS

For wooden fencing use 1,000-micron mount-board to create the posts and rails; these can then be wood-grained and painted before assembly. Paint the weathering and ageing after assembly.

To make the type of mesh fencing seen around playgrounds or factories, use the wire mesh available for car body repairs. It comes in sheets that will easily cut with scissors. Glue into position with fast-drying, two-part, epoxy resin and paint with enamel spray paints.

For iron railings cut one strip of 1,000-micron mountboard, 4mm wide and the length of the railings required. Cut a strip of 3mm foamboard to the dimensions of the footings that are being replicated. Measure and mark a centre line the length of the foamboard, then mark a series of points 6mm apart. Do the same with mountboard strip. For the uprights use cocktail sticks cut to the required lengths, leaving the point on one end. Make small holes in the foamboard to correspond with the points marked. Glue in the flat end of the uprights with quick-drying epoxy resin. Use another piece of 3mm foamboard under the uprights to support them as the glue hardens. Make 1mm diameter holes in the mountboard. When the base and uprights have completely set, push the mountboard down 5mm over the uprights. Glue into position by smearing some more of the epoxy resin on the underside of the cross-member and allow this to harden. The railing can then be spray painted with matt black car spray paint. For arrowhead finials, small blobs of contour-lining paste piped on to either side of the points are effective.

this will create differently sized stone in the wall. Begin at the base of the wall and cut and position individual stones (8 to 12mm in length) from the roll, allowing a small gap of 1mm between each stone. Vary the size and change the shape during assembly. Continue this process row by row up the wall. Alternate in the same way as with a brick pattern but allow the horizontals to waiver. Do this in stages, and so, after each roll has been used, mould the stones with the tip of the scalpel to heighten the roughness of the cut of each stone and pull some of the sculpting putty into the gaps and crevices. Occasionally add some small bits of putty as packing stones.

Once completed and hardened off, begin the painting by rubbing black gouache paint into all the crevices with a damp cloth; the epoxy putty will tolerate harsh rubbing. Add further colours in the same way until the colour and finish are achieved.

ROCKS

When creating a set with large areas of rock face it is important to obtain visual references

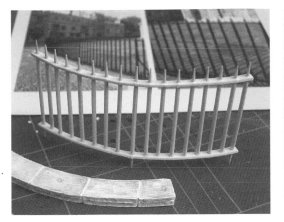

Part of a curved set of railings made from cocktail sticks and mountboard.

Above *Creating the rocks and structures for a model of the Minack Theatre, Cornwall, with styrofoam as the base material (student model-maker: Eve Lowrie).*

The finished rocks on the Minack Theatre model (student model-maker: Eve Lowrie).

for the geological stratification that might have shaped the environment. Use Styrofoam as the base material when building up the shape and the strata. Cut this with a hot wire or shape with a craft knife. With the basic shape complete, cover the surface with modelling paste or, for large areas, flexible household filler and leave to dry. Chip it away with craft knives, small chisels or modelling power tools to get the desired qualities. Paint with colour washes and sponging to make sure that the contours and recesses within the surface texture are fully utilized.

ROADS

Use a rough grade of watercolour paper to give the right texture. Paint with acrylic or gouache paint and then dust the surface with matt black and white spray paints to break up the paint effect. For road markings, mask off the lines by using masking tape as a stencil. Apply white or yellow emulsion paint with an artist's sponge. Dab most of the colour off on newspaper and then dab over the required areas. The lines should be sufficiently broken up and appear as if they had been rolled out. Make cambers with either modelling putty or a curved framework of mountboard and ticket card. The surface may then be spray glued over the top of the supporting structure.

SOIL AND MUD

Make loose soil from fine sawdust dyed in a similar way to that suggested for foliage, but this time use a black or brown cold-water dye. This can either be scattered loose or glued with PVA adhesive to preformed undulations. For the best results, apply the PVA adhesive to the surface, sprinkle the sawdust over the glue and gently pat down with an old paintbrush to make sure that the entire surface is covered. Knock the surplus off on to a sheet of newspaper and recycle.

For churned up ground, use terracotta, air-drying modelling putty and form the ruts and levels. Use water from a sponge to loosen the putty and make it more malleable and wet. Once dry, paint with gouache or acrylic paints

---

Exercise: Making a Quick and Effective Cobbled Street

Cobbled streets, in sheet form, are available from model stores. However, there is a simpler and cheaper method by using dried split lentils. Cover a section of 1,500-micron mountboard with modelling paste or gesso to a 2mm thickness. Sprinkle out the lentils on to a cutting mat and use the point of the scalpel to lift them up and locate them in the modelling paste, with the domed surface of the lentil showing. Allow the filler to set and paint the whole section with a biscuit-coloured emulsion. Then, with a burnt umber acrylic and a soft rag, rub the paint into the gaps between the cobbles. Sponge the stones with a variety of colours to get the right quality and variation.

A section of street showing the process of applying and painting split lentils to achieve 1:25-scale cobbling.

to replicate mud that has been sun-baked or paint with a mixture of gouache and PVA to create wet mud. Create puddles by filling ruts with clear adhesive and allowing it to set.

Modelling putty can also create arid conditions where the ground cracks. Roll out the air-drying modelling putty to 1mm thickness on a piece of brown tissue paper. Allow this to dry out completely. With a small hammer and nail, travel over the surface tapping the nail to split and crack the surface. The tissue will hold the pieces together so that the entire section can be glued to the stage floor of the model box in one piece.

SNOW AND ICE

If a scene needs to have snow settled on the set then create this by painting a thin coat of PVA on to the model where you want the snow to settle, then dust the model with icing sugar through a fine sieve. Allow the PVA to set and then knock off any of the surplus sugar. For trodden down or melting snow, model the contours with white, air-drying, modelling putty. Then apply a thicker coat of PVA with a light dusting of icing sugar; the sugar will melt into the PVA a produce a thawing snow effect. For discoloured snow, mix gouache paint with PVA before applying the sugar. This will give the effect of melting, slushy snow. If the snow needs to become watery then apply pools of clear adhesive. For the final addition, add a fine dusting of icing sugar to replicate newly fallen snow.

For frozen ponds or puddles paint a piece of mountboard to look like dark, muddy water by wetting the board and letting the colours bleed and flow together. Then with a mixture of white emulsion, PVA and water, create a consistency that is like that of single cream. Paint the surface with the mixture. Take a piece of tissue paper, scrunch it up and then flatten it out again; place it over the painted

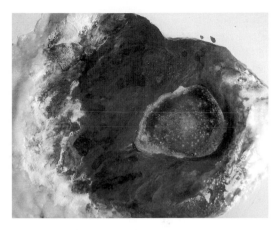

Sample showing frozen puddle and thawing snow as described below.

surface and smooth it out; carefully remove the tissue. It will remove most of the paint and leave a faint trace that looks just like the frozen surface of a pool. Clear adhesive squeezed all over the surface and allowed to dry will give a glass-like quality. When completely hardened, dust the surface with icing sugar by using a large make-up brush. Traces of the sugar dust will catch on the surface creating an icy opaqueness.

WATER

For standing water use either PVA or clear adhesive over a painted background, similar to the one suggested above for ice. If the water needs to be flowing from one level to another, then model the drop with fine strips of clear acetate glued into position. Complete the effect by letting a mix of PVA and white paint run down the surface of the acetate strips. Build this up in stages, similar to the way in which a candle drips its wax. The ratio of paint to PVA will depend on the speed of the water required: the faster the flow, the whiter the mixture will need to be.

6 FURNITURE AND FURNISHINGS

INTRODUCTION

When creating an interior or exterior environment the items that help to establish period, status and social background are furniture and furnishings. When audiences enter a theatre and take their seats they are unlikely to be sat in front of the house tabs or a front cloth. They are more likely experiencing an empty stage set in preset lighting. The designers and director have established an image that they believe is 'setting the scene'. With time to absorb what they see, the audience are tempted to create their own plot based on previous knowledge of the text, the playwright or the arrangement of objects within the space. With any performance there is always a history. Some action will have taken place before the play's first scene. Each member of the audience will be attempting to unpick the truth from the clues that are being presented.

Furniture selection and placement can play a large part in developing this line of communication with an audience, not only during the first moments, but also throughout the performance. Attention to period and

Opposite A selection of 1:25 scale furniture from various productions in a storage case.

character detail will help to maintain the illusion of a different time or place. The moment an item of dressing jars with its environment, the audience become unsure about the meaning of this anomaly and the illusion is broken.

When modelling furniture and furnishings it would be impossible to impart all the necessary details in such a small scale. However, the right choice of modelling materials and attention to period or style will communicate the desired atmosphere of the design and the intended quality of finish. In most instances, furniture and props are hired more often than they are constructed. However, a good model can make the choice of the appropriate hire companies, the condition of the furniture and the necessary colour schemes much more apparent. With the addition of photographic or pictorial references, the choices become clearer to those responsible for their sourcing.

When deciding on what furniture to model, make sure that you have all the information at hand. How will the actors use each particular item? Are there clues in the text or has the director said that he wants to be able to use the object in a particular or versatile way? Is the furniture of a standard size or might the proportions have to vary to fit its purpose within the production? These questions have to be addressed before a selection based on aesthetic or period qualities is made.

If the piece is set in particular period or about an historical figure, then further research on design movements, social history or visits to locations should be undertaken. The persistent problem in modelling furniture from paintings or photographs is uncertainty about what the back or the underneath of the item might look like. This may be important because on-stage action may mean that a chair is overturned during the performance and reveal its underside. Here the method of padding or strapping needs to be accurate to maintain the illusion of period. This becomes particularly important in studio venues where the audience are seated much closer to the action.

CHAIRS

A chair provides an actor with the opportunity to vary and develop different actions. Much can be read into the way a character sits in a chair. A chair can be a comfort or a prison, hurled across a room in anger or left empty as a reminder of an absent character. There are instances where chairs may be the only clue to establish settings, or may be as a device that the playwright uses to limit the need for elaborate staging, as in Alan Bennett's *Habeas Corpus*, where the script suggests that the staging is three chairs, or in the way that Ionesco uses chairs as both a necessity of the location and an indication of other invisible characters in his play *The Chairs*.

Above A selection of 1:25-scale upright chairs.

*Chair made from three sections of ticket card joined to create the appropriate thickness and allow for the insetting of the detailed back panel (*An Experiment with an Air Pump*).*

A 1:25-scale chaise longue, modelled with a mountboard frame covered in modelling putty with contour-lining paste providing the detailing.

Upright Chairs

When beginning to analyse how to make a scale model of a chair, look at the frame. How is it constructed? How can this structure be echoed in the way that the model is made? Use a wide variety of materials to ease the construction. The use of ticket card for the frame, strutting or panelling will be easier than cutting shapes out of thin, wooden veneers. Create the right thickness of legs, seats and backs by glueing two or three sheets of ticket card together, rather than using mountboard that begins to separate if cut too finely.

Turned legs can be made from beads strung on to piano wire or fine strips of masking tape wound around 2mm-gauge plastic rod or wooden dowel. Individual spindles sold in specialist model stores for staircases in dolls' houses, cut down and adapted, provide an accurate turned chair leg.

If the chair has curved legs these are best cut out of three sheets of ticket card, layered to create the thickness. Carving and feet can be piped on with contour-lining paste. Once this

mix of materials has been assembled to create the chair frame, it can be painted with a light brown emulsion paint to provide an even surface for the acrylic paint to build the final colour, graining and patina. If you are making a gilt chair use the same process except that you should use a terracotta red emulsion and

Exercise: Creating Scale Fabric

For more intricate patterns try scanning an image of the fabric required into a computer. Adjust the size in a drawing or publishing program and print out the image on to either white, high quality tissue or, for heavier fabrics, lightweight white fabric stiffener cut to A4 size. The printed item can then be cut into panels and assembled on to a chair, by using PVA adhesive. This printing method is also useful for marble or marquetry table-tops, but print this out on gloss or photo quality paper.

Pedestal table made from a combination of mountboard, ticket card and beads, painted with emulsion paint and a coat of mahogany wood stain (An Experiment with an Air Pump).

then spray or paint the frame with gold enamel paint. If lightly applied, some of the red will show through giving the chair more depth and authenticity. The seat is best made from modelling putty and painted to replicate the chosen fabric.

TABLES AND DESKS

Tables are invariably large items of furniture that may occupy a lot of stage space and so careful consideration of their size and purpose is essential. What has to be set on the table? What weight must it support? Does anyone stand on it during the performance? How many place settings are required? Is the size or height going to cause sightline problems for an audience? An example of a table where the size is crucial comes in the play *Arcadia* by Tom Stoppard; here the table has to accumulate various props and belongings scene by scene, nothing is struck (taken off stage), but characters still have to be able to work on it throughout the performance.

The modelling of table-tops is best done in ticket card. Use double-sided tape to fasten layers of card together with slightly different dimensions. This will create the mouldings that appear around the edges of some period tables. A frame to hold the legs is usually located under the table top. Model this in mountboard to give rigidity for positioning the legs. Make the table legs by using a similar process to chair legs. Shop-bought, dolls' house spindles have the perfect dimensions for turned legs. Where a table has pedestal legs, model these with a combination of beads, ticket card and plastic or wooden dowelling. Assemble whatever combination of these best matches the particular furniture style. It will be useful to make a drawing of the pedestal before you begin to model it. Prime the finished table with light brown emulsion and finish with acrylic, gouache or specialist scenic paint, to match a particular wood or graining. For highly polished tables use a clear gloss varnish or wood stain.

For desks, fascias and drawers made of ticket card can be added to the underside of a table-top. The handles may be added by piping contour-lining paste on to the centre of each drawer in a fine line, or, for more ornate handles, 0.5mm-diameter copper wire can be painted gold, cut and bent into shape and then located on the drawer by piping gold contour-lining paste over the ends to create the fastenings. If a leather surface is required, mask off the edges of the desktop with masking tape. Select a gouache paint mix that is of the right colour and then mix in equal parts of PVA adhesive. Paint on to the surface of the desktop and, while it is still wet, stipple with a stencil brush to create an uneven surface. Once dry, peel off the masking tape to reveal the leather-trimmed desktop.

Metal Chairs and Tables

Use 1mm copper wire for chairs and 2mm wire for tables. Copper is the best metal to use because it can be easily formed and soldered to create the desired style and then spray painted with the appropriate metal finish.

SOFAS AND EASY CHAIRS

Begin the internal structure of these by making the shape with mountboard. Cover the structure with air-drying, modelling putty sculpted to create the padding and cushions. Once this has dried, then paint patterned fabric on to the putty with acrylic or gouache paint. If, as the putty dries out, it separates from the mountboard frame, glue back in place with clear adhesive Alternatively, print the fabric on to tissue paper and cut into pattern sections and glue into position with spray adhesive. Apply the adhesive to the tissue paper and then smooth out the cut pattern on to the model. The tissue will overlap easily to create neat edges. Make turned feet or castors from small beads. Where an easy chair or chaise longue has a frame, make it in the same way as the frame and legs on a table by using the method previously discussed.

CABINETS, CHESTS, DRAWER UNITS AND WARDROBES

These structures tend to be more set dressings than interactive objects within the perform-ance. They can, however, add to the character and sense of period being portrayed in the staging. It is much more likely that they will be hires rather than makes, and so the time spent in modelling should be proportionate to the needs of the particular production. The models may be simply used as a reminder when sourcing furniture.

Make most of the structure with ticket card since it will form curves as easily as flat panels. Glue clear acetate sheets to the back of a cut frame of ticket card to create glass-fronted doors. Drawers can be simple rectangles glued on the surface of the piece. For handles, knobs and carvings use contour-lining paste. Constructing the furniture in a

A 1960s armchair made from a mountboard frame covered with modelling putty; the antimacassars were cut from a lace trimming.

87

ticket card that is close to the required wood effect will reduce the time spent on wood-graining.

If wardrobes are to be opened then a door can be left ajar and the clothing inside modelled by draping tissue in several colours, soaked in an equal mixture of PVA and water, over a scale hanger made from 0.5mm copper wire. Mirror card can add detail inside the door.

BOOKCASES

Given the number of plays written concerning literary figures or language it is not surprising that libraries and bookcases become a popular scenic element. With a play such as *Educating Rita* by Willy Russell, the bookcases become a metaphor for the development of Rita and the decline of her tutor Frank.

Modelling the bookcases and shelves is a simple task best achieved with 1,000-micron mountboard cut to size and assembled. If the bookcase contains central uprights then cut and slot these together. The books themselves can also be individually cut from the mountboard, painted down one edge to create the spine and then glued together to create a row that fits on to a shelf. The covers of the two end books will also need to be painted. More covers may need to be painted if the shelf is randomly stacked, or the books are loose or stacked in small piles.

Pictures, Frames and Mirrors

Cut images for pictures from magazines or download from the internet. Reduce these to size and print out on photo quality print paper. Assemble the frames over these prints. Make simple wooden frames from ticket card and paint to suit. For gilt frames, follow the same procedure and then apply gold contour-lining paste piped into the design required. Once dry, age this by painting burnt umber gouache or acrylic into the recesses of the detail. Mirror card, purchased from artists' suppliers and mounted to the back of a frame, will create a wall mirror. Mirror card may also be scored into or cut into individual tiles to create a mirror-tiled wall.

A set containing a wardrobe made from a combination of mountboard and ticket card, painted to tie in with a painted gauze (Shadowlands; Sutton Arts Theatre).

Row of books having their spines painted before being located in the bookcase (Educating Rita model; student model-maker: Kerry Shepherd).

CURTAINING AND DRAPES

When modelling curtains and drapes one of the main problems is to get the folds and the fabric to hang correctly. A quick and effective method is to fasten aluminium baking foil to the back of fine fabrics such a silk organza or chiffon, thin cottons or tissue paper by using spray adhesive. The fabric will then drape as required because the baking foil will keep the folds in position.

For heavier fabrics, soaking in PVA adhesive may be a better option. Use a mixture of one part of PVA adhesive to two parts of water. Soak the fabric in the mixture and then squeeze out all the surplus. Drape the fabric into a chosen style and set it aside until it is completely dry.

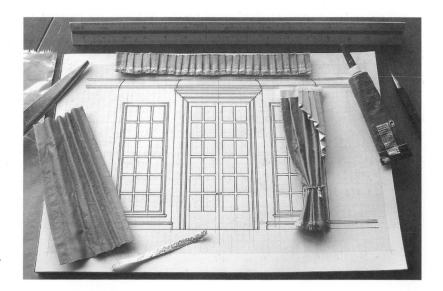

Drapes and pelmet made from silk organza backed with baking foil to help to retain the folds; detail added by using a contour-lining paste.

The sceno-graphic model, showing kitchen units made from plastic box tubing and mountboard, spray painted silver and covered in metal finish card (The Kitchen; *designer:* Nicholai Hart Hansen).

For curtain poles, use 2mm plastic rod or wooden dowel. Cut the material to the required length and add beads to create the finials. Paint as a wood or metal finish. Glue the finished curtains to the underside of the pole. Add curtain rings by glueing small strips of metallic thread to the top edge of the curtain, passing them over the pole and glueing them to the back of the curtain.

Tie-backs can be created with platted embroidery threads or bands of the same fabric–baking foil combination. Make tassels by grouping together twenty strands of embroidery threads 100mm in length. Take a small piece of thread and tie a knot around the bundle close to one end. Trim the ends as close as possible to the knot. Take a 2mm-diameter bead and, with tweezers and clear adhesive, glue the knotted ends into one of holes in the bead. Take another piece of thread and knot it around the bundle 5mm down from the bead. Cut the threads just above this new knot. Shake and you will have the completed tassel. The other threads remain fastened together to begin the process again.

For tablecloths, fasten tissue paper to the tabletop with double-sided tape. Then brush a mixture of PVA and water around the overhanging paper and arrange in draped folds.

KITCHEN ITEMS

Make most equipment, cupboards and surfaces in a similar way to the previously mentioned cabinets and tabletops. Use white ticket card or gloss card for all 'white goods'. If the appliances are of stainless steel, use mirror card dulled down with an application of matt glaze. For an aluminium sink and drainer, use the metal foil packaging that scalpel blades are supplied in. When reversed, the colour is a good match and the material can be bent and scored easily. Fasten edges together with clear adhesive. Use the same material to make pots and pans. For ceramic sink units, sculpt them from oven-firing modelling putty; 1mm copper wire bent into shape with a small bead mounted on the top will replicate taps.

BATHROOM EQUIPMENT

For baths, whether freestanding or boxed in, use the oven-firing modelling putty. The smoothness of this medium creates the sleek curves required. Feet for a free-standing bath are best made separately and glued on with clear adhesive before being painted. Use white gloss spray paint to get the ceramic finish. For tin baths, work out a pattern in paper first and then cut the sections out of copper sheeting. Then curve, shape and solder the sections together. Once complete, the tin bath can be spray painted silver.

Toilets vary in construction depending upon the period of history. In Victorian times the cistern was mounted high on the wall and supported on ornate brackets, and the toilet bowl was probably made from blue and white porcelain or had floral or classical details moulded into white porcelain. For the cistern and bowl, again use oven-firing modelling putty. For the wall brackets and seat, use ticket card and paint to suit. The piping should be formed from 2mm-diameter copper or brass tubing. Make the bends necessary by using long nose pliers. This size of tubing should bend without folding. Create the pull chain with 0.5mm-diameter piano wire with a bead glued to the end of it. The modern toilet has so much of its structure hidden that the bowl, seat and handle may be all that need to be modelled.

The same techniques as have already been explained are used with sink units. The cabinet or supports may vary, but they may all be made from ticket card, painted to look like iron work, melamine or wood.

BEDS

Beds can be very individual items of furniture. Much of the character or personality of the owner is evident in the bed's shape and condition. The state of the linen and additional props will have histories or stories of their own; Tracey Emin's installation art piece, showing her own bed during one period of her life is a prime example. What is important to establish is how the bed is or has been used. Does the bed need to be double, three-quarter or single? Does the bed have to be sprung to create bounce? Is there enough room for a full-sized bed? There may be opportunities to

1:25-scale model of a Victorian toilet in situ; the cistern and bowl are made from oven-firing modelling putty and the pipe and chain are copper wire and tubing, the rest is cut-card and paint.

foreshorten the length or distort perspective if the bed is viewed end-on.

The basic structure can be a simple mountboard box; but it is what goes on above that gives the character detail. Make pillows and sheets with thinly rolled modelling putty. Roll the putty out to 1mm thickness and arrange either neatly or unkemptly over the base. Make the pillows with the same putty, leave to harden and then glue in position with clear adhesive. Make the covers or throws from fabrics backed with baking foil and then drape or dress over the sheets.

Canopies and posts can then be added. As an example, for the posts on a four-poster bed use 0.5mm-diameter piano wire and thread and glue beads and plastic tubing to create the

A partly made, four-poster bed showing the use of beads on piano wire to form the posts (student model-maker: Kerry Shepherd).

design required. Further detail can be built up by piping contour-lining paste on to the beads. The posts can then be primed in a suitable base colour emulsion paint in preparation for the final painting or wood-graining finish. Swags and draping should be fastened to each cross-member, made from 1,000-micron mount-board, before assembling the four sides to create an open box around the posts. The whole bed can then be assembled with the use of suitable adhesives. Further details such as cords and tassels can be added once the structure is complete.

PRACTICAL LIGHTS

For scenes that take place in the evening, it is useful to have a physical source that the light

could be emanating from. It can also be an indication of ceiling height. Within the design it is necessary to establish the presence of the lights, although it is not essential that they actually work. However, with fibre optics and small, battery-operated novelty lights it is now possible to provide light within the model, but, like the performance, it will need to be supported by additional specials when photographing or presenting the scenographic model.

Crystal Chandeliers

Begin by making the metal supporting structures out of copper wire soldered together to match the number of arms or bands. Build any solid structures by threading beads and modelling putty on to the copper frame. For filigree work, pipe contour-lining paste on to the structure. White tubular beads 8 to 10mm in length make ideal candles; paint before adding the crystals.

To make the strings of crystal use the type of fine beads used on beading dresses and string them on to measured lengths of fine silver thread. Glue the candles and the strings of beads into position with cyanoacrylate glue. For crystal chandeliers that contain domed shapes and long strands of crystal substitute 3 amp fuse wire or 0.5mm piano wire for the silver thread so that the strings of beads hold the correct shape.

Candlesticks

For single candlesticks use 0.5mm piano wire and thread and glue beads to create the right contours; leave 5mm of wire extending from the top and spray paint the candlestick with the appropriate colour. Then glue a white tubular bead for the candle on to the end over the wire that has been left. For multiply-armed candlesticks, solder 0.5mm copper wire around a central core strand, in this way beads can still be threaded over this core strand to create the body of the candlestick.

Above *Practical lights designed as supporting columns, with the whole height illuminated to emphasize the 1930s interior décor* (**Present Laughter**; *director: Angie Langfield; lighting designer: Simon Benison; actors: Tim Steed and Georgina Mackenzie*).

Overhead Lights

These are again a useful signifier of period, be they candles, gas or electric. Suspended above a set they can provide a key source for the lighting design within a scene. In preparation for making the light fittings it is always useful to save clear plastic caps from bottles or tubes. These are useful for constructing lights that contain domes or jars. An opaque, oven-baking modelling putty is available which can be moulded to create glass shades. Shape and solder the framework with copper to fit the required design and then spray paint the required colour. For the chain that suspends the light use a piece of 1mm piano wire; this

Sliding glass beads on to lengths of fine piano wire to create the crystal strand for the top section of a chandelier.

will keep the light fitting stable and reduce any swing that might make setting or flying the light into the model difficult.

STREET FURNITURE

Where an exterior location is only a small scene within the design or text then items of street furniture may be all that is necessary to establish the scene. With the help of lighting and sound, an area of the stage can become a street or a park linked by the way in which the actors will use the space and the furniture.

Park Benches

It is usual for park benches to show their own history: they are open to the elements and maybe rain-washed and rotting or bleached by the sun with peeling paint, they may have been vandalized by the characters that are using it. Thought should go into the decisions about the look and the quality of the bench.

Bench and waste bin modelled as a truck assembly (The Cosmonaut's Last Message to the Woman He Loved in the Former Soviet Union).

The struts on a bench are one of the few instances where the use of wood veneers works. Because most benches are weathered and broken-down by use, the scale of the graining is helpful. If graffiti are required, add these with an airbrush or fine marker pens. The supports could be of wood, concrete or metal; use a mixture of ticket card and mountboard. For concrete, use mountboard and apply and stipple gesso to create the right texture.

Telephone and Pillar Boxes

Scenes quite often require an actor to be on a public phone, and again, the way in which the telephone box is distressed can give a clear indication of where it is located. It is unlikely that it will have all its glass, it may have been used as a toilet or even as someone's home.

To make the basic structure use ticket card, and remember to paint and finish the frame before adding the glass. The windows and doors can have clear acetate fastened to the back or, in the case of the door, sandwiched between two fascias. Make the curved roof section with modelling putty over a ticket-card frame to get the smooth contours. Type and print the telephone sign on a computer and glue into position with a small section of clear acetate spray mounted over it. Make the inside detailing, such as the telephone, with oven-firing modelling putty and glue into position. Once the box is painted its pillar-box red and distressed to suit the design, glaze the outside surfaces with PVA.

For the body of the pillar box use the 'column technique' and cut a strip of red ticket card to the correct height of the box and 150mm in length. Find a piece of dowel that is of the correct diameter and roll the ticket card around the dowel, using double-sided tape to fasten the end in place. Use black electrical tape wound around the base to create the bottom section. Make the other detailing such

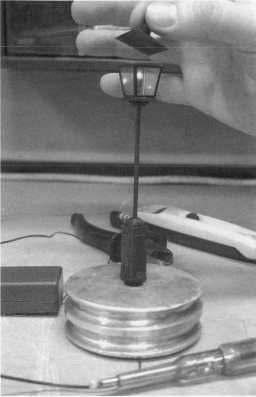

Above *1:25-scale telephone box and pillar box made from ticket card and clear acetate (student model-maker: Kerry Shepherd).*

Street lamp made from brass tubing with a rice light fitted and illuminated (model-maker: Mike Bell; practical lighting: Ian Bald and Nick Paddy).

as the letterbox and door from the same red ticket card. Sculpt the top from oven-firing modelling putty; paint and glue into position with clear adhesive, then glaze the outside with PVA.

Street Lights
When establishing an outdoor scene at night one the most useful items of street furniture can be a street light. This may by physically present or a lighting effect, but it can provide a useful means of lighting a character in a particular way to support the mood or location. The lighting designer usually supplements the light from the lamp itself by adding a lighting state to enhance and give more control over what the lamp is illuminating.

It can add drama to the model presentation if the lamp actually lights up. This can be done quite easily by isolating a single strand from a set of rice lights (battery-operated, interior design lights readily available at Christmas time from interior design stores). Make the post from plastic of copper tubing then the single light may be fed down the tube, with the battery pack and switch located under the floor of the model. Build the rest of the structure around this tube with ticket card and modelling putty. If the street lamp has an arm, use copper tubing for the post and arm and then solder the two together. Spray paint the lamp-post before adding acetate sections for the glass.

7 THE SCALE FIGURE

It is most important to include the characters right at the beginning of the design and model-making process, but there is always the temptation to launch straight in with staging ideas. Analyse the empty model box first before building any environment. The theatrical space might be quite small or, conversely, voluminous, so to experiment with the relationship between the actors and the stage might lead to a more reasoned design proposal that fully utilizes the resonance of the theatre space.

THREE REASONS WHY SCALE FIGURES ARE NEEDED THROUGHOUT THE DESIGN PROCESS

They Give the Designer a Means of Direct Connection to the Theatre Space

In the initial stages of exploring the actual theatre space, the designer has become engaged with it through the plans and, wherever possible, a site visit. It is now necessary at this stage to identify what qualities the stage or the theatre space itself has. These could be inherent in the shape and the texture of the structure, or possibly personal resonances with what this space represents. The subsequent chapter explores the creation of the theatre model box. When this is complete, the need exists to reaffirm that personal connection with the theatre space through the placing of a figure or figures in the empty model box.

A Scale Figure Provides a Means to Measure All Other Aspects of the Design

In life we create environments designed to fit with our personal needs and shapes. In the theatre we maybe copying, abstracting or challenging these environments, but we are always creating a playground for the actors and the action. If a designer/model-maker makes the set user-friendly or, conversely, difficult for the actors to work with, it is always a deliberate decision. Treads for stairs have a particular height and width for ease of movement. Seats have an established height from the floor to make sitting easy and posture correct. Tables and desks have functions and need to be of the right dimensions for the desired action to take place. Doors are of particular heights and widths for human activity. We are constantly qualifying spatial surroundings in relation to the human body. So, by first creating an accurate scale figure, a designer is able to identify and articulate all this instantly in the model box.

Opposite 1:25 scale figures made to portray some of the characters in **Vassa.** *Student designer: Lesley Read.*

Using scale figures to create a dramatic moment and experiment with the space required by the actors (Romeo and Juliet; student designer: Marielena Kapotopoulu).

Exercise: Self-sculpture

If the first scale figure a designer makes is of him or herself, then by placing this in the empty model box it becomes a scale representation of the designer in the actual theatre space. It provides the visual link between his or her initial responses and the design challenge ahead. It becomes logical to want to view the space from that figure's perspective. Get pictures, by using a digital camera, of the designer from the front, the side and the back. Use these as reference to sculpt the figure. A full explanation of sculpting techniques appears later in this chapter.

A self-sculptured figure placed in an empty model box when first considering the qualities of the space (student designer: Becky Gunstone).

In the design and model-making process it is important that designers constantly remind themselves of their responsibility to the actor. If a designer has a figure standing in the space, then as soon as he adds suggested staging, there is an immediate analysis of scale and relationship to the figure and consequently to the actor. Figures can also be 'walked' around the model by the designer and the director as they look at how scenes can be developed and blocked.

A Design Must Include the Figures in the Same Way as a Play Includes the Actors

When designing for the theatre, a designer must always remember that his or her work is never viewed by the public as a piece of installation art. The performance is the final goal and this performance involves the actors' relationship with the text, the acting space and the audience.

If a design model appears complete without the scale figures that represent the characters, then in some way the characters and the play have become superfluous. A designer has allowed the model to tell the complete story and not given space for the text or the performance. This might be less likely to happen if scale figures are included from the beginning of the design process; a model without figures should somehow feel and look unfinished.

The characters must have their role and personality built into the design process. There are always questions to be asked about the relationships between the characters and the space. Who has ownership? Are the characters at one with their environment or are they alien to it? How much of the characters' personalities is inherent in their environment? Do you need to show status between characters? An easy way of addressing these questions is to make scale representations of the actual characters alongside the development of the staging. Then, when finally the design is presented to the actors, they have a direct means of connecting with the set. They can superimpose themselves on to these scale characters and imagine themselves inhabiting the space. This does not mean that a designer has to make exact copies of the actors, that would be extremely difficult and might appear to exclude, rather than include, them in the designer's 'world'. But the

The sceno-graphic model for Educating Rita, *Oldham Coliseum Theatre (model recreated by student designer Kerry Shepherd; scale figures by student designer Becky Gunstone).*

The use of a cut-out chorus to establish scale and the space required in the model of the Minack Theatre.

figures should have a quality of the characters they signify and, wherever possible, be clothed to match with the costume designs.

GETTING THE STANCE AND THE POSTURE RIGHT

To get accurate, interesting and relevant posture into your scale figures take a series of photographs of a suitable person from different angles in the position that you require. A digital camera is useful here since it can speed up the processing. Then display these in your work area when modelling the figure. Try to clothe them in something that represents the final costume so that you can work with the qualities of the fabric as well as the figure's proportions. For example, if she has long clothing, you may not need to spend time modelling legs that are not seen. If you want characters to interact in the model you could use this method and pose people in the photograph to suit the moment of interaction.

DIFFERENT TYPES OF SCALE FIGURE

There are several different ways to achieve a 1:25-scale figure. The choice of which type may depend on what a designer feels secure in making or it may be a time or quantity issue. Whichever method a designer chooses, scale and proportions are the most important factors: these should be as accurate as possible. If the body proportions are wrong, then what appear to be suitable sizes for levels and furniture within the model, once built, become out of proportion with the actor. By then it is often too late and the only solution may be to cut elements from the final staging.

THE CUT-OUT

The simplest form of figure is a silhouette cut-out. This can be made quickly by sketching out the shape on a piece of black mountboard and then cutting around the outline with a scalpel or craft knife and mounting the silhouette on a small mountboard base. The cut edges are best blacked in with a permanent marker. For a more sophisticated version, select characters from the drawn costume sketches or by looking through copyright-free magazines and books for reference images. Reduce these to the appropriate scale and adapt them to create the right qualities and character.

This is an immediate method that may be useful when creating entire choruses or if the design is for a promenade performance where there is a need to include the audience in the finished model. It may also be that time is too limited for alternative methods. Cut-out characters are useful as a preliminary stage to enable the designer to make quick references to the characters in the space and then from these develop more sculptured forms as the staging ideas develop.

One of the drawbacks to this method is that the figure is only a two-dimensional representation and so lacks the capacity to fill its space in the same way as a fully sculptured character would. It might be difficult to make an accurate judgement concerning the space that the action might require. It is also difficult to make a seated cut-out look effective on a three-dimensional chair. Furthermore, this type of figure lacks weight and can be unstable when one moves characters during presentations of the design. Finally, if there is an intention to record the scenes photographically for a storyboard, the figures become more difficult to light.

SCULPTURED 1:25-SCALE FIGURES

The drawbacks that exist for a two-dimensional scale figure become the attributes that a fully sculptured, three-dimensional figure has. Here the touch, look and stance of the figure can be an accurate representation of a moment within the performance.

There are several methods and materials that designers or model-makers use when creating these figures. However, the principles to follow are similar to those of a sculptor: begin with an armature, then use a quick method to give the body parts their shape, finally, add details such as skin, hair and clothing. The choice of materials or even of methods may be determined by the style of the production. If all the characters in the play stem from a natural landscape within a design, then a more rough-hewn quality might be most suitable. However, if the design is for a costume drama then a more refined and intricate finish might be required.

Armature

Time spent getting a good and accurate armature will make the later stages easier. Make sure that the proportions are right and that the scale is accurate for the character or actor. Remember that this is the first stage and that several layers will subsequently be added. Allow for this when shaping and sizing the figure. The gauge of wire to be used will depend on the size and the stance that needs to

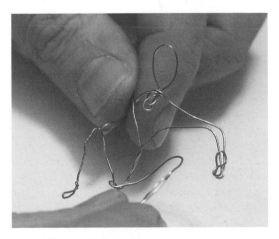

Making the wire armature for a scale figure.

be modelled. Choose one that provides the right level of manipulation and support. If a figure is 'caught in action', then a thicker gauge will help to support the figure when adding the flesh. Choose a gauge of wire that can initially be twisted and shaped with the fingers (0.5mm). To get the structure of the hands and feet use a small set of pliers.

Bulking Out

The next stage is to add the rough contours of the body to the wire frame. A quick and effective way of doing this is by using aluminium foil. Tear small strips and apply them to the frame. The foil covers easily and can also be pushed and compressed to fit the shape you are trying to achieve. It is also flexible enough to allow further positioning of the arms and legs, and even when applying the final layer the armature remains flexible until the skin and the clothing have hardened. The profile is the hardest view to get right

when making a figure. Cut out a silhouette in card of the side view of the character you are modelling; this cut-out can then be used as a gauge to check scale and posture as you model.

Skin, Hair and Clothing

When the basic structure of the figure is complete, it is time to add the finishing details. There are several types of modelling putty that can be employed to create skin and features. Each will have its own qualities when sculpting: the air-drying kind is the most readily available and, once it has dried out, can be sanded or scored into to create the appropriate finish; it can be difficult to create fine detail because of its fibrous texture and it also will begin to harden quickly from the warmth of the model-maker's hands. The epoxy compound putty is smoother and has a more sticky quality. This stickiness can be lessened by wetting the putty as it is sculpted;

Adding aluminium foil in small strips to bulk-out the figure.

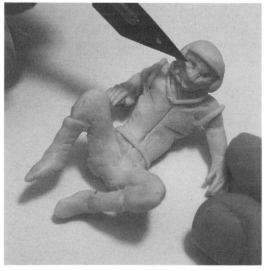

Applying and sculpting oven-firing modelling putty to complete the figure.

Exercise: How to Create Accurate Faces

The face is undoubtedly the most difficult object to model in 1:25 scale. This simple method can create a stock of faces that may be applied to figures as and when required. Spend sometime modelling a male and a female face so that they are as perfect as you can make them. When they have hardened, press them into a flat block of modelling plasticine as far as the ears. Do this as many times as you like. Then take some dipping latex and, with the end of a brush, drop a small amount of latex into the plasticine moulds, fill halfway and then tap the block to release any trapped air and allow time to harden. Once hardened, the latex will change colour from white to ochre. Then add the next level of latex until it just reaches the edge of the mould; if filled to this level when dry it provides a perfect concave back to the face for attaching to the figure. To release the face, bend away the plasticine and the face will pop out of the mould. For the final skin tones use matt enamel paint since this will stick to the latex without filling in too much of the detail.

Filling a face mould with dipping latex.

Breaking open the plasticine to reveal the face cast.

this too can be sanded and scored once it has hardened and it probably provides the most robust finished figure. The third type of putty is one that you harden in a domestic oven; this has a smooth quality when modelling and will roll out extremely finely to create fingers and even braiding on clothes and is available in a wide range of colours to enable the modeller to create skin, hair and clothing in colours close to the required ones; this may reduce the time taken when painting the final figure.

FINISHING TOUCHES

With hair and clothing, a wide variety of materials can be utilized. One method is to use modelling putty to create both hairstyles and clothing, which is then painted up with gouache, acrylic or watercolour paints. Some watercolour paints are transparent and, when painted on to modelling putties, give a more natural look with highlights and shade and the ability to build up layers of colour.

1:25-scale figures of the cosmonauts inside their capsule **(The Cosmonaut's Last Message to the Woman He Loved in the Former Soviet Union).**

Some model-makers prefer to use tissue paper to create clothing. Use a watered-down solution of PVA glue; apply the tissue paper to the figure, building in the folds and details by pushing the tissue paper around with the point of the scalpel blade. This will allow for the movement and spaces that exist between the body and some elements of clothing: an example might be a crinoline or period costume worn with a cloak.

Wigs and hair can also be made by tearing tissue paper into small strips. Scrunch these up with PVA glue, mould the tissue paper either on to the model figure's head direct or apply a thin layer of cling film to the model first; this will allow hair or wigs to be constructed so that they can be removed or changed.

When considering clothing for model figures an obvious choice might seem fabrics. However, it is difficult to find fabrics that match the appropriate scale and will hang and drape on the body in a manner suggesting the qualities of the costume or clothing. Silk organza or fine woven muslins may work well, but these will need to be soaked in a watered-down solution of PVA to both stick to the figure and artificially create folds and drapery. Avoid using samples of the actual material of the clothing fabric to be employed in the production: they will be of the wrong scale and bulk out the frame of the character too much. This will lose any posture or detail that has been so carefully sculpted.

When the scale figure is complete, a matt varnish may be used to seal any paint that might be water-soluble. This will both enhance the colours used to paint the figure and make the figure more durable. A designer rarely keeps every full design model that he makes, but figures can be used continually. Additional changes can be made to the period, the character or the colour of clothing by simply modelling and painting over an existing figure. Alternatively, store the figures away and over the years build up a collection. This will enable future experimentation with designs that are associated with large casts, or provide the immediate opportunity to place a suitable character in the model box. Of course, the designer has the option of buying 1:25 scale figures direct from specialist shops and then painting them up to match his other designs. Although expensive and fixed in limited poses, they will always look accurate and professional when placed in the model.

SCALE FIGURES PROVIDE THEATRICALITY

Whether a designer chooses to buy or to make figures, they are still a crucial element to the process of creating the design and the finished scenographic model. An empty stage may be exactly how the designer and the director

The use of tissue paper for hair and clothing on the figure of Mrs Lovett in Sweeney Todd.

envisage the final performance. This reference to an empty stage is unlikely to refer to the actors, the lighting or the sound. This minimalist approach may the more easily be explored through the positioning and playing with lighting on the scale figures in the model box.

If theatre design is about finding new meanings or illustrating the themes we do not necessarily hear immediately from a text or a score, then the figure in the model box portrays more than just the actor or the character's physicality: it represents what has been already been established about the particular piece of theatre before any new enquiries that the director and designer are about to embark upon. It is unlikely that any performance will exist on stage without an actor, singer or dancer, and it is for this reason that accurate scale figures are key to the success of a scenographic model – they add the theatricality and without them the model will have no real sense of performance.

8 DEVELOPMENTAL STAGES OF THE SCENOGRAPHIC MODEL

The previous chapters have explored the different items that can exist within the scenographic model. When approaching each new design there are various types of model that, through their development, can enable the designer to engage personally with the chosen text and space and provide a useful tool for communication with the director and other members of the design and production teams. First are the initial models that explore and experiment with the space itself, using the designer's and the director's dramaturgical responses and research around the subject or text. The ideas from these are then honed and shaped within the making of the final scenographic model, where both the realization of the creative vision and the technical and financial requirements combine. Before any design process can begin the designer has to create the theatre model box, the 'blank canvas' that will enable him or her to pursue future enquiry.

Opposite *Fully finished scenographic model that accurately defines the space and contains all the aspects of the design needed by the production team* (An Experiment with an Air Pump).

Theatre model box of the Cottesloe Theatre, South Bank, London.

CREATING THE THEATRE MODEL BOX

This model box includes all the architectural details that may affect the manner in which the designer uses the space within the design. It is crucial that the model is accurate within the selected scale: any discrepancies will persist throughout the design process and detrimentally affect the final scenographic model, providing false information to all concerned. The model should include the performance space, the wing space, the backstage, the proscenium and the tower height (where relevant) and the seating. The last is particularly important for studio spaces where the configuration of the audience to the

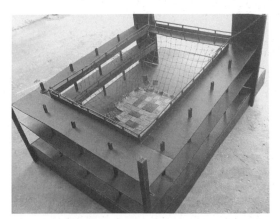

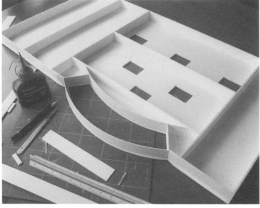

Using a compass point to prick through the ground plan and into the foamboard, following the internal dimensions of the theatre space.

Strutting and strengthening the underside of the model box.

space and the performance may be a design decision.

Before beginning to construct the model box, it is important to consider the opportunities and limitations that exist within the actual theatre space. These include all the entrances and exits. When cutting out the walls, leave the doorways as voids to begin with; this will give an opportunity to check the arrival or removal of the set and props from the space during fit-up or interval changes.

Is there an under-stage? If so, model this depth as it may provide future entrance opportunities. Make sure any contours and equipment that sits proud of the internal walls of the space are included in the model box. These include fire appliances, which will also require easy accessibility at all times, and emergency exits, which in a studio space may have to remain illuminated throughout a performance.

Study the ground plan and the section drawings of the given space. These should contain all the necessary measurements and information concerning both the technical

and the architectural properties of the space. Where at all possible, a visit to the venue can assist with any queries concerning the theatre's specifications. Photographs taken of the backstage area will give the designer/model-maker the possibility of recreating more of the resonance and texture that exists within the space; this is of particular importance where a design uses an open stage.

Use 3mm foamboard for most of the structure of the model box. This material is light and holds its shape well, without bowing when spanning large areas of walling. Begin by draughting out the floor plan on to a sheet of foamboard. Take the theatre ground plan and position it on top of the foamboard, taping it down to maintain its position. Then, with a compass point, pinprick through the plan into the foamboard, registering all the points along the inside dimensions of the space. When the plan is removed, join up the pinpricks with pencil lines to reveal the floor plan. Before attaching any of the walling, create the substructure to the stage. Decide on the depth necessary and, in foamboard, create a surround and the internal struts to suit that depth. If the stage floor already has traps, make sure that the strutting accommodates this. The traps themselves should be pinpricked and carefully cut out of the floor, labelled and kept for future use.

When building the walls, begin by making the proscenium wall, or, in a studio space, the walls that contain the exits. It is possible to build the model box so that all the walls are in slotted sections that link together and then locate into the stage floor. This makes the model box collapsible for ease of carriage. For further details on this method refer to chapter 8 in *Stage Design: A Practical Guide* by Gary Thorne. The following method results in a fixed structure.

For proscenium venues, begin by measuring off the section view all the necessary heights to which to build the theatre walls. Check the height that you want the flying bars to be set at; do this by checking the sight lines from the front row of the auditorium on the section view. Make sure that the walls of the model are at least of this height. The proscenium wall is the only one where it is important to model the exterior and the interior dimensions. This will enable the wall to be free-standing and

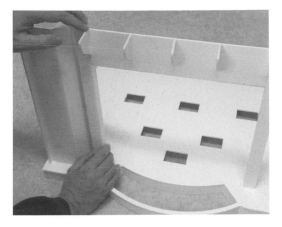

Beginning to fasten the individual sections of the proscenium arch to the stage floor.

indicate the depth of the proscenium arch and the correct position for the header and the iron. Simplify the detailing that exists around the front of the proscenium, unless this detailing is an integral aspect of the design. If it is, add this later in the design process.

Once the proscenium wall has been constructed and glued into position on the stage floor, build the other walls to meet this to complete the model box. Once each section of

Avoid Foamboard Meltdown

Since foamboard is attacked when certain adhesives are applied to its edges, it is best to use a PVA wood glue which provides a strong bond and does not eat into the foam. However, this glue takes several minutes to bond, so hold structures in place by using bobble-headed dressmaking pins until the glue has hardened; but when fastening flat sheets or strips of foamboard to each other use double-sided adhesive tape.

Allow for Lighting the Model

In the side walls of the model box include removable sections to provide opportunities for cross-lighting the model once the design is complete. Sections of these side walls may also be made to include clear plastic inserts, which will achieve the same result; it can be difficult to get any dimensional lighting into a model that has three solid walls. With these removable sections, experimentation and photography become more feasible.

wall has been measured and cut out but before assembly, add any structural details such as brickwork, piping, flying cages and doors since these may be difficult to add once the walls are complete. Additionally, fasten two strips of foamboard to create ledges set at the same height and width as the fly floor. These should run up and downstage at right angles to the two sidewalls. Add a photocopy of the bar positions, directly from the ground plan, and glue to the top surface of these ledges. This will provide accurate positioning for the flying bars when the staging is included in the model box.

Add triangular struts to the outsides of the back and the side walls for further support and to keep the walls vertical.

Once the model box is complete it should be spray painted matt black. This accepted format provides a contrast between the design and its surroundings and establishes a clear difference between the proposed design and the existing theatre space. The proscenium arch can be extremely ornate with strong colours and textures, but, unless this is an integral aspect of the design, these details should remain matt black. To avoid the spray paint eating into the foam infill, glue strips of black ticket card over any exposed edges of foamboard before spray painting. As a final addition, black, self-adhesive felt can be applied to the front proscenium wall. This gives a clean, dense black finish that will cover any imperfections and reduce any shine that might distract when lighting and photographing the finished model.

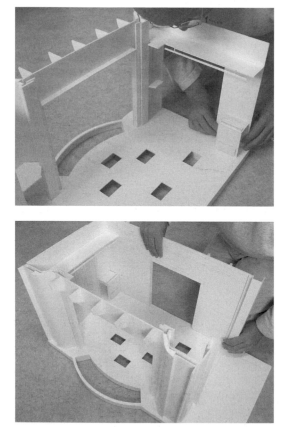

The finished model box spray-painted matt black with final details such as doors and flying bar references added; on this model the flying cage has been made from open mesh to enable the model to be lit from stage right.

Attaching the other completed walls once the proscenium is in place.

INITIAL MODELS

In the early stages of a design it is important to keep options open for as long as possible. It is in these first days of experiment that the models need to be fluid and immediate. After thorough text analysis, the making of the initial sketches and the collecting and disseminating of visual research have been done, the next stage is to give this research form and shape. One method of doing this is by a series of sketch models. These, as their name suggests, do not require high levels of accuracy and finish. They are quickly formed approximations of the theatre space that allow a designer to be adventurous and playful when testing out ideas.

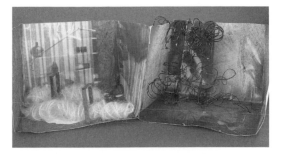

Two free-form sketch models exploring the qualities within the text by using found images from colour magazines and material scraps (Il Pagliacci; student designer: Michelle Douek).

SKETCH MODELS

This type of model is the initial response, a stepping stone to future developments. By experimentation with shapes, textures and colours, this model can translate and develop ideas from the first thoughts and renderings in a sketchbook into something directly spatial.

Black ticket card, held together with clear adhesive tape, can quickly create an approximate studio or proscenium model box. The scale at this stage can be approximate but should be proportionally correct. Depending on the size of the venue, choose to work in approximations of either 1:50 or 1:100 scale.

The sculpting of the space can be modelled by using white ticket card, with the details sketched out with pencils or marker pens. Photocopies of architectural elements or landscapes can provide immediate representation; some of these could be selected from research or cut out of magazines. Modelling clay can create more organic shapes and surfaces. The use of scissors instead of knives will speed up the modelling process and encourage immediacy. It is probably best to begin work in black and white so that silhouettes and shapes that cut across or change the space are more obvious. Gradually replace these with colour as ideas develop.

Three sketch models prepared to explore different staging possibilities from a single design idea (Il Pagliacci; student designer: Helen Dufty).

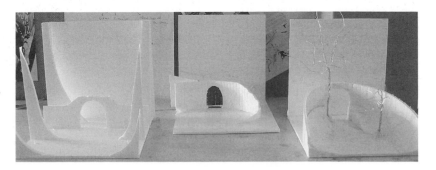

Quite often a designer will have more than one idea for a design and not know which to pursue. Sketch models offer excellent opportunities to create three-dimensional sketches of ideas before the final selection is made. The very process of making the models may help the designer make that choice or provide the opportunity to offer several possibilities to a director. When a production has more than one location or scene, then a series of sketch models can provide a three-dimensional storyboard, a quick means of plotting movement and transformation.

The sketch model also gives the director the chance to contribute to the shape of a design at an early stage in the process. Sketch models can provide clearer examples of how a designer is intentionally sculpting the space than two-dimensional visual references or sketches can, which, though accurate and accessible, can never fully capture spatial ideas. Directors also think spatially when examining and exploring the text. Sketch models provide a common ground for joint experimentation. At this stage in the process, designer and director feel able to make significant changes or completely reject ideas without themselves feeling either rejected or dominated.

The sketch model can provide the necessary confidence and assurance that come from the knowledge that certain spatial and aesthetic decisions are understood, before a white-card model is begun.

WHITE-CARD MODEL

This type of model, although still experimental within the theatrical space, has a higher degree of accuracy and scale than the preceding ones. It is the first model that will come under the scrutiny of more than just the designer and the director.

This model exploits the theatre model box and experiments with design suggestions within the accurate scale version of the theatre. As its name suggests, the model is made in white card that contrasts with the black theatre model box. This clearly identifies what elements are design additions and how, through the consideration of scale, shape, mass, line, balance and composition, the development of a design proposal grows.

As the design moves from the smaller sketch model to the larger scale theatre model box, some of the ideas that have been played with may need only slight adjustment or may open up completely new lines of enquiry. Before

---

Begin Technical Drawings Alongside the Design and Model-making Processes

Drawing seating blocks and the acting area on to the ground plan of the theatre at this early stage will give a much clearer appreciation of the floor coverage and of the relationship the seating has to the acting area, including sufficient space for gangways and emergency exits. Even in the primary developmental stages of the design process, it is beneficial to explore ideas both in the model and on the ground plan simultaneously. Do this by placing a sheet of tracing paper over the ground plan that has already had the seating added. Draw on to this any design ideas as they develop then change and attach new sheets of tracing paper as and when required.

A finished white-card model for a studio production showing how the choice of seating configuration has dictated the shape and structure of the design (Blasted; student designer: Nichola Sawyer).

transferring any design proposal from the one to the other, begin by placing a scale figure in the empty theatre model box. The reason for this was explained more thoroughly in chapter 7. How will this figure enter and exit the space? Where are the strongest acting areas? How will the audience view the performance? These questions need to be answered before other design elements are included.

Placing the model on a stand at head height makes it possible to view the acting space from the audience's perspective. From this angle sightlines and the placement of the audience become easier to address. If the audience are seated, is this seating already fixed or is flexible and capable of being positioned to best suit the concept for the performance? Does the audience have a choice of where they want to sit, or are they promenaded around the space? Referring back to the text analysis, research and initial thoughts (sketch models) and contrasting these with the space will help in the making of creative, objective and practical suggestions.

With an experimental or flexible studio space the decisions made concerning the seating or the audience's view are an integral aspect of the design concept. Thought must be given to how an audience should feel when attending the performance. Are they to become part of environment? Are they merely observing the action, or is there some level of audience participation? The audience could be in a single block (end-on) or be able to observe each other's reactions during the performance (thrust, in-the-round, traverse or promenade). The qualities of each should be considered against the text and the space before a final decision is made.

If the audience is raised on tiered rostra or raked then make simple blocks in black card to represent these. This will help to define clearly the acting area in the model box. Build these blocks to house the correct number of seats and comply with safety requirements for gangways and access to emergency exits. The theatre may have recognized configurations

Experimenting with found objects in the theatre model box, while listening to the score and letting the mood and orchestration dictate the arrangement (Il Pagliacci; student designer: Mic Kemp).

A rough, white-card model prepared for a second meeting with a director (Il Pagliacci; student designer: Helen Dufty).

and expected audience numbers; these should be ascertained and incorporated from the start.

It is important to consider the audience's positioning carefully in these early stages since the stage shape that this creates may enhance or restrict the movement of the play. Qualified decisions may avoid last-minute changes being imposed on a design by theatre management whose responsibility is to the paying public and the safety regulations, and not the aesthetics of the design or the performance.

Even though the creation of this model is now in scale, try to maintain the freedom and fluidity that were possible in the sketch model. When beginning to develop the staging do not be tempted to fix ideas too soon. Begin with scraps of card and found objects that can represent shapes and forms for the staging.

Found objects can be a useful way of challenging the space. These might have certain qualities that the designer feels are important to the structure of or the meaning

held within the text. These could exist within the quality of the material, its texture, its shape, its colour or its mass – any or all of these may contain resonances of the text for the designer. It is unlikely that these objects will still exist in the final design, but traces of them may appear or the objects may provide a link to the final design concept. Move the objects around, trying them at different sides of the space, at different angles and in different sizes. Always view them in relation to the scale figure. Accidental positioning in the model box can create new possibilities, but only if the designer keeps an open mind and is not simply recreating a preconceived design idea.

Only when the shapes become more essential to the needs and the vision of the design should fully formed white-card structures be made. Use the scale rule to draw out every piece; it will give an understanding of what the item is going to mean in actuality. An expandable steel rule is useful to check the scale against the real dimensions. It is easy to make levels, treads and walls that look true to scale but could prove an acting challenge once scaled up to full size. Remember that a white-card model, although still an approximation of the final design, needs to meet a certain level of accuracy. The designer may need to provide an indication of materials and overall sizes for costing or directorial reasons.

As the structures become more tangible, add architectural details such as stairs, windows, doors and traps. These are essential in establishing how an actor is seen or how he gets access to the several areas of the stage, such as second-storey levels. How does an actor get up to the second level? Is it by a sweeping staircase or a vertical ladder? Is the window in the right position for both the action and the lighting opportunities? Which way do the doors open, are they self-masking or will they need to be masked upstage of them?

The designer alone cannot answer most of these questions. They have an impact on the work of the director and other designers in the team. The development of the white-card

*A white-card model meeting between designer and director (***Absolute** Hell; *director: Angie Langfield; student designer: Louise Watson).*

model is the perfect time at which to involve their combined creativity.

The director and the design team now have an opportunity to discuss and provide the necessary input to make the design a shared vision. It is at this stage that questions concerning the positioning of lights and sound should become an integral aspect of the design. The lighting designer or the sound designer will have his own ideas that he wants to bring to the production. These may have an impact on the height of the staging (to get the correct beam angles) or allow for the inclusion of 'practicals' within the staging itself. Being a blank canvas, the white-card model allows the lighting designer an opportunity to suggest possible colours and lighting effects, including how particular shades or textures could be deployed before colours or textures are added to the model itself. The lighting designer may also want to use side, back or top lighting, so the stage designer may have to adapt the design to allow for these. The sound designer will want to see what the space is going to become visually so that he can heighten the

Beginning the Working Drawings

As shapes and forms develop in the white-card model, remember to take some quick reference drawings of the technical data. Do this by drawing around the elements with a 2H pencil. Do this before assembling the different fascias as fully formed structures. This may be much easier than trying to take measurements off the final scenographic model. Add overall sizes to these quick technical drawings since they may become the preliminary drawings that provide the main reference when completing the final working drawings.

illusion with the sounds that are developed or composed.

Theatrical masking should be discussed at this stage. Does the lighting designer want the rig on view or hidden by legs and borders? If the latter, how intrusive will this be within the space and can the masking be designed to become part of the total concept? The sound designer will also need to discuss speaker positions in conjunction with the masking, since the piece of theatre may make particular demands for sound to appear from specific places or objects within the set. As the technology improves, speaker sizes are being greatly reduced, but the stage designer may still have either to accept that a speaker will be visible or find a way of disguising it within the design.

In theatre today the possibilities for creativity and the improvement of quality within the design of the sound and lighting are growing rapidly, so the need for these elements to be included early in the design process is becoming crucial to the general quality of the performance. Today there is a movement towards more fluid staging that includes storytelling with projections, sound and light,

so the white-card model marks the perfect time for the creative team to come together to push boundaries and try new ideas.

The white-card model is also the stage at which the production manager, the technical manager and the stage manager may become involved. It is important that, before proceeding on to the final model, the designer knows the costs and the technical implications that the design creates. The design may be too expensive to produce or may have elements that technically become difficult to achieve within the time allocated. Of course, in an ideal world the designer is fully aware of all such factors and always designs within budget, but reality is never quite that simple. The designer/model-maker should look on this contact time as an opportunity to let these people have their creative input.

Offering up the white-card model to scrutiny and others' creative input during its development allows the final scenographic model to become an artefact with a shared understanding and ownership among the entire design team. This is important as it enables the designer/model-maker time and the opportunity to concentrate on the

---

Getting the Technical Drawing Complete at the White-card Model Stage

Once the white-card model is complete but before moving on to create the final scenographic model is the perfect time to complete most of the technical drawings. The white card model should end as an accurate scale representation of the intended design, so disassemble it or measure from it to provide all the necessary technical information. Compare earlier preliminary drawings with the model and use the former or their data where appropriate. It may also be a good opportunity

at which to check the sizes and structures against the architectural aspects of the theatre space by plotting them on to the ground plan and section view. As a final check, photocopy the drawings, mount them on to mountboard and cut out and assemble them to recreate the white-card model. These sections of the model will form the basic structure ready for the application of texture and colour that are required in the finished scenographic model.

accuracy and the precision required to encapsulate the qualities that the design requires.

THE FINISHED SCENOGRAPHIC MODEL

It is in this model that the information has to be exact, perfectly in scale and provide the production team with all the necessary facts concerning the design, both aesthetically and practically. To achieve this it is important to analyse carefully and predict what the design should look like when in production. Remember that the scenographic model is a reference artefact and not a work of art. It is possible to be swept away with the process of model-making for its own sake and not fully consider how it should appear when scaled up.

It is crucial that the model is of a standard of finish that enables the other members of the production team to deploy the information specific to each one's speciality. This requires that the model should:
- be accurate in an appropriate scale;
- contain all aspects of the design that are to be constructed;
- be coloured and textured appropriately;
- be able to demonstrate working aspects of the design;
- contain all entrances, exits and get-offs; and
- contain the furniture that the design requires.

Be Accurate in an Appropriate Scale

Final scenographic models must be in perfect scale. The scale used will depend on the size of the venue but is most frequently 1:25. The attention paid to scale should also include the textures, architectural details and furniture. The construction team, scenic artists, prop makers and stage managers will all take their own particular measurements and direction from the model.

Experimenting with light to see the possibilities and problems that arise from using a mirrored stage floor (Il Pagliacci; student designer: Seema Iqbal).

Contain All the Aspects of the Design to Be Constructed

Any aspect of the design that requires building rather than hiring or sourcing must be included in the model. The model gives the construction team a clear indication of the quantities and qualities that are required to enable them to plan for the on-coming build. Any items not included may affect the workload and endanger deadlines. Items for construction should also include large props, such as specially designed furniture, tableware or lighting.

Be Coloured and Textured Appropriately

It is only in the final scenographic model that full colour and textures appear. These particular aspects of the model are crucial to the scenic artists who will sample and create treatments direct from the model. Some textures may appear appropriate in a scale model but when enlarged to full scale become

An example where the structure and the stylized design needed to be fully realized in the scenographic model to give clear instruction to scenic constructors and artists (Little Shop of Horrors; Oldham Coliseum Theatre and national tour).

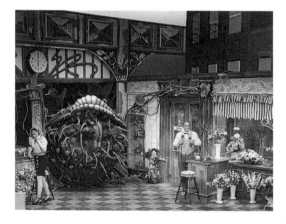

A production shot from Little Shop of Horrors, with Sarah Lancashire and Jeremy Brook, showing the level of accuracy achieved by the scenic artists in translating from model to production (Oldham Coliseum Theatre and national tour; scenic artists: Celia Perkins and Mathew Jones).

Example of a model to demonstrate how the set has been designed to show the destruction that occurs within the text (Blasted; student designer: Jane Barker).

clumsy and too bold. Careful analysis of what a scaled-down paint treatment or texture should be before applying it in the model might eliminate later confusion.

Be Able to Demonstrate Working Aspects of the Design

When creating the final model, consider within the structure and the making of the scenic elements how the staging moves and transforms during the production. This may mean making multiple sections of the staging that show how set pieces change to reveal or create new locations. This may be as simple as two sets of drapes, one open and one closed, or a complicated manoeuvre where trucks, raised flooring and flying pieces conjoin. Fasten cloths and flown flats to piano wires suspended across the top of the model box. Use dressmaking pins to locate them in their position on the flying grid. These may have labelled tabs added to the centre of the top edge to identify each flying piece and provide an easy means of manually controlling their flying during presentations.

Contain All Entrances, Exits and Get-Offs

It is important to include not only the entrances and exits that exist within the staging but also how these relate to the ones within the theatre itself. Are they concealed or open and do the audience and actors use the same entrances? The model will be scrutinized to make sure that the passageways are adequate and that clear emergency exits meet all safety standards. Make sure that get-offs from raised levels of staging are made and positioned accurately within the model. It is important that the actors and stage management know how they gain access to the stage and whether these are by treads or ladders, which may alter the timing of entrances and exits. Remember too that it will be dark backstage and so get-offs should be a made as simple and as clear as possible.

Contain the Furniture that the Design Requires

It is important to model all the furniture that appears on-stage, not just the items that are to be constructed. The actors and stage management need to understand how crowded or sparse the stage is to be to help when blocking each scene. It is also useful for stage management to see the level of set dressing that is required so that they can plan for sourcing, storage and scene changes.

The levels of finish and how to achieve the specific stage items are covered in chapters 3 to 6, and how and why the final scenographic model is important to the rest of the production team is covered in more detail in the chapters that follow. However, the most important feature of this model is that, through its development and final appearance, it provides a direct means of revealing to others something beyond appropriateness. The fact that the model is a perfect scale representation and that it addresses the practicalities of the text, space and time are only the fundamentals. The scenographic model should surpass these and truly express a collaborative vision, demonstrating the excitement, the challenge and the potential that the design has to offer. This is more difficult to define and label. In essence, the individuality and creativity that occur during the problem-solving and modelling processes are what personalize a design. If a model-maker were asked to recreate a scenographic model from working drawing and photographs, that model is unlikely ever to fully achieve the qualities of the original. It needs the full creative process and personal involvement to capture its true essence.

9 RECOGNIZING PRODUCTION AND CONSTRUCTION IMPLICATIONS

THE PROPERTIES OF THE ACTUAL STAGE

Throughout the design process, the theatre model box is a constant resource for the structure and the volume of the space. However, the space itself has certain given properties. For example, it may have one or a series of traps in the stage floor. What is the access from the under-stage and how easily are the traps opened from the stage level? The theatre may also have stock items such as cycloramas, gauzes, borders and legs, and the masking of all of them could be a requirement within the design and the model, but only if the information and specifications are gathered at an early enough stage in the design process

When designing for a venue it is important to study the theatre plans and equipment lists thoroughly to gain a complete understanding of the equipment, properties and access that the space has to offer. This may become even more significant if the design is for a tour where the staging will need to fit more than one venue. When analysing the information

Opposite *The making of a pub bar directly from the 1:25 scale model (the model is shown in the foreground).* The Cosmonaut's Last Message to the Woman he Loved in the Former Soviet Union. *Student constructor: Colin Mander.*

gleaned, pay special attention to the following properties: an awareness of these can provide for a more coherent transition from the model to the build and fit-up in the theatre space.

Dock Doors or Main Access Doors to the Stage

Do the doors lead directly off the street, are they at the same height, or are the doors above street level? Does any stage scenery have to enter the space through more than one set of doors or have a corridor to negotiate? What size are these doors? All these questions need to be answered to make sure that the construction of the staging is done with prior knowledge of the access to the stage. These dock doors are usually the main access point, *so all elements of the staging must fit through them.*

Lighting and Flying Bars

How many does the theatre have? Of what type are they? The quantity and age of such equipment can vary tremendously between venues. The designer will take no part in the decision concerning the selection of venues for a tour. Tours quite often include venues with widely differing characteristics, from full flying facilities at some theatres to others with limited flying or none at all.

It is important during the white-card stage of the design process to allocate suitable lighting and flying bars to ensure the correct

121

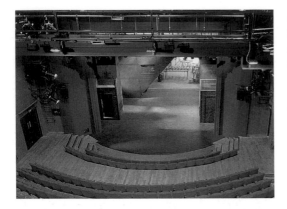

Dock doors open showing access between the workshop and the stage (Central School of Speech and Drama).

positioning and loads for cloths or flying pieces. The grid is shared with the lighting designer who may need specific bars to obtain the correct lighting angles. During the design period it may sometimes be more advantageous to move the on-stage set to fit with a flying piece and its bar than to alter a bar that is essential for lighting.

When making decisions, check which type of bar it is and whether it is suitable for the intended purpose. Winch bars are slow moving and best designated as lighting bars. The use of counterweight bars is essential when flying large items of set where the weight needs to be distributed to make it physically acceptable; Heavy items of set may need more than one bar. Hemp or counterweight bars can be used for lighting; the choice will depend on the number of lamps hung from them. Cloths can be flown on either hemp or counterweight.

Fly Floor
It is important to check what height these are above the stage level. Are there lighting bars, booms or heating ducts fastened to the underside of the gantry that change the

available height? Large sections of flattage may need to be cut to fit around these obstacles, which may not appear on the theatre drawings.

Stage Management Position
The usual position for the stage management prompt desk is stage left. But certain venues have it set on stage right (known as 'bastard prompt'). Although with cameras and monitors most of the cueing is done from the screen, some technically challenging designs may require the deputy stage manager (DSM) to have a clear view of the stage. Even so, the DSM and the desk will occupy some wing space.

House Tabs
The designer has to decide whether the house tabs fit with the design concept or are 'flown out', with the audience viewing an open set. Whichever it is, it is unlikely that the theatre will want to remove them to free up the bar.

The Iron
The theatre iron is there to protect the audience in case of an on-stage fire. As a safety regulation, it has to be seen in operation once during each performance. This can be done before the show or in the interval, but it could also be part of the design concept; some are quite neutral in appearance and the sound and movement associated with them can be atmospheric under the right conditions and design rationale. When designing the set, remember that the line on the stage floor where the iron rests has to be clear of set and furniture and that, if a false stage floor runs under the iron-line, it must have a section built into it that creates a firebreak.

Legs and Borders
Theatres will have a stock set of legs and borders that can be employed by the designer.

When model-making it is important to check the sightlines to make sure that the arrangement of these masks the wings and the lighting grid to create the 'black box'. Make sure that this arrangement also allows access for any trucks or large items of furniture that need setting.

Masking

As a more interesting design opportunity, create legs and borders to extend the design concept beyond the acting area. This will avoid the harsh edge where the set becomes the wings. An extension of this would be to design and make the model so that parts of the actual stage structure become self-masking, or the angle at which the sets sits on the stage automatically masks the wings on both sides. Quite often, any consideration of masking is left until the end of the design process. This either compromises the look of the staging by creating a hard line between the on-stage set and the wings, or its position can interfere with possible lighting opportunities.

Dip Traps

Dip traps exist at the sides of stage to carry electrical cabling up and down stage safely and neatly under the stage floor. Be aware of these. The crew may need to have access to these traps, so sections of the set or false flooring may have to be removed quickly to make it possible to get at this cabling when problems arise. Outline these on the model with a 0.1 black ink pen.

Stage Traps

Traps provide the opportunity for another form of dynamic entrance from below the stage floor. The theatre may already have these as permanent fixtures or have flexible, structured flooring which enable the designer to choose the location. Traps can also be present within levels that the designer has

built into the stage set. The simplest is a hinged trap that opens on to the stage; this will usually open upstage to create an instant 'reveal' as an actor climbs out. Access is usually by ladder or steps. A grave trap is a motorized trap to raise objects or actors up to the stage level at a pace similar to that of a body rising out of a grave. A star trap is also motorized but moves much quicker for speedier entrances; calculate the

*Model from above, showing how a gap has been left where the iron line is situated (*The Kitchen; *designer: Nicholai Hart-Hansen).*

Example of how the legs used for masking can be an integral aspect of the design (Habeas Corpus; Oldham Coliseum Theatre).

required measurement for the traps to include an excess of at least 200mm to allow for slight misalignment. Designing mesh or Perspex tops will give the opportunity to use light or smoke to add to the stage effect.

Hydraulics

Hydraulic rams and lifts can be effective methods of raising and lowering entire sections of the set or flooring. The designer should discover what the under-stage technology looks like, so that the set design will either be in sympathy with the equipment or need additional elements of staging will be to disguise it. Hydraulic staging has similar safety requirements to automated traps and so actors will need time to familiarize themselves with the equipment, and may even have to be clipped to the structures by chains before certain movements are undertaken.

Rakes

The term relates to stage floors that are set at an angle. Rakes can aid upstage sightlines or create an unbalanced ground in relation to a design concept. Set and furniture may have to be anti-raked to maintain verticals and avoid doors swinging open or catching on the floor as they open. Some theatres have built-in rakes. It is important to check this carefully with the theatre since a built-in rake may not be apparent from the theatre ground plan. If designing a rake for a set, test out the angle in reality: what may seem a gentle incline in the model box can become a mountain slope when experienced at full size. A practice rake, set up in the rehearsal room, can ensure that the actors' moves and timing are established on the rake and not the flat rehearsal room floor.

Scenographic model showing the use of a raked stage in a studio space (The Storm; student designer: Claire Elcombe).

A revolve bisected to allow for changes to the set when in the upstage position (The Secret Rapture).

Revolves

Some stages have built-in revolves, otherwise specially constructed or hired revolves can be erected on top of an existing stage floor. There are full-circle or ring revolves; with full-circle revolves the entire surface can rotate in either direction; with ring revolves the centre and the outside ring can operate independently to add further choreographic possibilities. They can be a convenient way of changing scenes when there are multiple locations. The staging can be built on to the revolve with different scenes occupying different sectors. Each scene can then revolve around to the front when it is required. This attribute can be utilized more creatively by designing staging structures that are less segmented and create a more composite staging that, when turned, reveals different aspects of itself that can become the separate scenes. The revolve is particularly useful when the production has an in-built sense of travel, with actors moving from one scene to the next while the revolve is turning. It is always best to use a revolve sparingly because an audience will soon become bored by a production constantly on the move.

When modelling a revolve it is not essential that it is motorized, but it should move freely with a finger or a scalpel point. Use an attachment for a compass set that can accommodate a scalpel blade for the accurate cutting of circles. Use 1,000-micron mount-board for the top and the bottom surface, with strutted supports inside to create the desired depth. Fasten a piece of high gloss card on the base of the revolve and the floor of the model box to reduce friction. Make sure that the central pivot is perfectly positioned or the stage revolve will catch against the walls of the surrounding floor as it turns. Make the surrounding stage floor to the same height and by using the same materials and strutting as the revolve itself. It is best to cut the circle in the surrounding floor 1mm larger in radius

Example of a motorized truck big enough to contain a small scene and several characters, the motor being cleverly concealed under a crate (My Mad Grandad; director: Warren Hooper; lighting designer: Phil Clarke; Oldham Coliseum Theatre).

than the revolve itself to allow for any slight misalignment. Check that the revolve turns freely. If it does catch, then smooth areas out with fine-grade sandpaper. A pop rivet fastened through the floor of the model with its surplus spike facing upwards will create a firm pivot for the revolve to be fastened to. Alternatively, a long dressmaker's pin will provide the axis and can be easily pushed through the layers of card.

Trucks

Trucks, either motorized or manual, can carry large sections of set that need to be relocated or move around the stage space during the production. These can follow set tracks laid into the floor or be more fluid in their movement. They can have directional wheels set to run in one plane or multidirectional castors for varying the positioning on stage. For the model, a simple mountboard box with a foamboard base will suffice. Calculate the

depth, taking into account the internal structure and the wheels or castors. If the truck is on a track, cut a groove with a craft knife in the track-line on the floor of the model. Feed bobble-type dressmaking pins from under the base of the model box, through the track and into the truck base; these will locate the truck in position on the track.

Trucks may also be an integral part of the stage floor. They can extend the full width of the stage and form horizontal, moving bands within the structure of a false floor. This allows items of furniture or characters to enter or exit in a horizontal path across the stage. These may be motorized or manual and useful to create horizontal transitions between scenes, when the beginning of a new scene is entering as the old one is struck. Multiple floor trucks make possible the setting and striking of scenes in more than one direction at the same time.

Model these as strips of stage floor that extend into the wings and sit between two fixed sections of flooring. When presenting scene changes in the model, place the furniture on the portion of the truck that is off-stage and push it into position.

UNDERSTANDING THE CONSTRUCTION AND BUDGETARY IMPLICATIONS

The responsibility for the construction and painting of any staging may not reside with the designer/model-maker. However, it is essential that they should have a clear understanding of the implications that their designs have on both the costs and the practicalities of any necessary build.

The scenic constructor will expect that a designer will provide him with technical drawings taken from the model that give all the measurements necessary to make it possible to complete his own working drawings. It is important that the designer has an awareness of the construction techniques and materials that are both suitable and fit with the budgetary constraints.

This information can have a direct impact on the building of the model. If a designer has this information, then the sizes and qualities of materials can be included in his decision-making and in the manufacture of the model itself. The designer will also have confidence that what he is asking of others is feasible. A scenic constructor will work primarily from the technical drawings. During the planning and building there will be occasions when the design has to be reinterpreted or adapted to make the staging physically possible. However, a change in construction that might seem small and insignificant can have an immense impact on the aesthetics and the manner in which the actors use the set in performance. It is necessary that the drawing and the model communicate the design concept in full. Information in the technical drawings must contain all the necessary technical data; but by virtue of being only lines and measurements, they cannot necessarily capture the

Exercise: Knowing the Materials

Suppliers will readily provide catalogues and price lists. A designer should build a file that contains these and other relevant notes about possible applications. The file should include the following categories of suppliers of:

- batons and sheet timber in soft and hardwood;
- architectural mouldings such as beading, skirting board, architraves, dado rails and large profile mouldings;
- steel in sheet, box, rod and mesh, and copper sheeting;
- acetate sheeting;
- door and window furniture, including; hinges, catches, door handles and knobs, key hole covers and finger plates;
- hardware such as fixed-wheel and multidirectional castors, pin hinges and brakes;
- the full range of scenic paints, plasters and glazes.

A model and the numerous technical drawings required to build the final staging for Sweeney Todd *(drawings drafted by Dean Clegg).*

qualities of the complete staging. The constructor will continually refer back to the model for verification. Only together do the model and the technical drawings give the complete picture.

UNDERSTANDING THE NEEDS OF THE SCENIC ARTIST

A scenic artist will use the model more immediately, matching both textures and colours when preparing samples for the designer's approval. There should be a constant dialogue between the artist and the model, checking that what is being enlarged to full-scale empathizes with the concept and the qualities apparent in the design model.

The designer can ease the sampling process by providing the scenic artist with the visual references used to create the particular designs or paint treatments; a record of the paints used

on the model (specialist scenic paints, wherever possible) and additional samples of specially created treatments that he can study closely without having to dismantle the model.

UNDERSTANDING THE PROP MAKER'S ROLE

The scenic prop maker may use the designer's model less directly in his work, since items that the former has responsibility for may not exist in enough detail within the scenographic model. However, in the construction of stage properties he may make his own scale maquettes and working drawings before creating the full-scale version. This scale model will need to embody the aesthetics already established by the designer. Therefore the designer should consider putting together a reference pack or resource sheet that includes a design sketch, showing how each item will be

Scenic artists measuring and analysing a backcloth in preparation for ordering the canvas (scenic art tutor: Sue Dunlop; students: Mabel Colleredo Mannsfeld and Tony Eden).

Scenic art students working direct from 1:25-scale artwork to create a full-scale, painted sky gauze (scenic art students: Mabel Colleredo Mannsfeld and Natasha Shepherd, Central School of Speech and Drama).

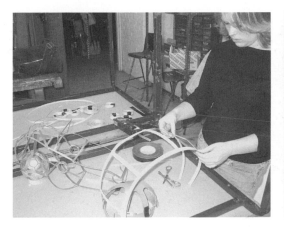

Using a large-scale maquette to test out ideas before making the final prop (Equus; student: Ellie Goldsmith).

Above *The author with the scenic construction team discussing the building of the ship for* The Odyssey, *with a 1:10-scale model (workshop supervisor: Alex Turnpenny; student scenic constructor: Colin Mander).*

used in performance and visual references of similar items to provide the prop maker with as much background information as possible.

When discussing the scenic makes with constructors, scenic artists and prop makers, it is important that the designer should have a clear rationale for his or her choice of a particular treatment or product. There may be a range of suitable materials but they could have very different properties when in production. Keep a materials diary, listing each product and its use on a particular production, as a resource to support design decisions. This may become particularly useful when the interpreters make suggestions based on a supplier's recommendations or costs but the designer insists on a particular material because its potential on stage is understood.

The designer is unlikely to be available for continual consultation with the construction team. Therefore the scenographic model, accompanying drawing and references have to carry the weight of responsibility for the communication of the design concept – they have, in a sense, to speak for themselves.

The finished ship in 'full sail' in the production of The Odyssey *at the Minack Theatre (students on the BA Drama and Applied Theatre Course at the Central School of Speech and Drama).*

10 LIGHTING AND PHOTOGRAPHING THE MODEL

LIGHTING THE MODEL

It is most important that the consideration of possible lighting states should take place throughout the designing and the model-making process. In an ideal situation, a lighting designer should be part of the creative process from the first discussions with the director through to the finished scenographic model, then the quality of light as a means of enhancing a dramatic moment or scene, and opportunities for sculpting the space with light become an integral part of the design.

If the lighting designer is not employed until the later stages of the design process, then the set designer/model-maker must take on some of his or her role and experiment with the possibilities that light can offer.

Then the quality of light as a means of enhancing a dramatic moment or scene and opportunities for sculpting the space with light become an integral part of the design.

Even in the early stages, during the placing of random shapes of white card within the model, light can have an impact on the decisions about structure and position. The selection of any light source will always be out

Opposite Using an angle-poise lamp to give the impression of light streaming into a run down palace. **Twelfth Night** *at Dundee Rep; Designer: Tom Piper.*

of scale with the model and more powerful than any conventional theatre lamps. Therefore experimentation with light at this stage should be free from the characteristics of specific lamps. One of the strongest and simplest sources of light available is obviously natural daylight: position the model on a sculpting stand so that daylight is coming from one direction, then simply rotate the model, watching for interesting shafts of light and the play of shadows.

Following on from this first experiment, consider the possible directions that light might emanate from –

- top light: projects directly down on to the stage and characters, used to add dimension;
- back light: light that comes from up-stage will create silhouettes and add further dimension;
- side light: light that is directed from the side of stage across the space, useful when capturing movement;
- front light: light from the front of house, levels should be set with other on-stage lighting to avoid flattening out;
- footlight: upwardly directed light, 'cabaret style', lights the characters harshly and creates dramatic shadows;
- below stage light: light that can emanate from traps or mesh/acetate floors that will up-light characters.

Above Using a single overhead light to create depth and shadows; showing how light can enhance the model where the staging is minimal (Romeo and Juliet; student designer Tom Curtis).

Using a focusable torch to light a particular character on the model, creating a dramatic moment on camera (photographic storyboard for The Cosmonaut's Last Message to the Woman He Loved in the Former Soviet Union*).*

One of simplest ways of exploring these possibilities is to use a focusable torch. These can be quite small and so to move them around the model and position them in tight areas becomes easier than with conventional torches or mini spotlights. Do this in a semi-darkened room to view each lighting angle in isolation. Change the size of the staging elements and entrances in the theatre model to see what effect this has on the shapes and corridors that the light creates. Doing these experiments alongside the creation of the set design will automatically create space for light to exist both physically and artistically within the model, and therefore the subsequent, finished production. Without allowing an

appropriate space for light, any set design could lose its dramatic potential and there may be no way of achieving the necessary angles or positions to light the space effectively.

When creating surfaces within the model also observe how reflective they are; if a floor or wall surface has a high gloss or consists of a mirror, it will create bounce (this is where light reflects off the floor and creates spillage on to other areas of the stage). Also consider how well light can be isolated; as a rule, the darker and more matt the surface, the greater the opportunity to contain the light within a desired area of the stage.

Try to build into the design as many options for lighting effects as are practicable. Some dramatic lighting states that happen in the final production may be lucky accidents, but they will be possible only if there is inbuilt flexibility within the choice of colours and textures.

PHOTOGRAPHING THE MODEL

There may be several reasons for needing to photograph the scenographic model, each will serve a slightly different purpose. With a photographic storyboard, each scene needs to be shot from the same full stage angle, with characters and set fully lit to show the layout and accurate positioning. Portfolio shots will require dramatic lighting that creates moments within the staging, and for photographs with which to discuss possible lighting ideas with a fellow designer, the photography needs to concentrate on the variations that occur in the different lighting states.

Exercise: Colour and Texture

Following on from the establishment of the basic structures in a staging proposal, experiment with how light can change colours and textures. Create some samples and arrange them on different planes to test how the light affects their surfaces.

Use a Rosco or a Lee swatchbook of samples to test a variety of filters: place a filter in front of the torch beam and observe what effect it has on the samples. Try preparing samples formed from more than one colour or texture; as an example, in the case of wood-graining consider making the treatment by using primary and secondary colours rather than a premixed brown, this will allow differently coloured lights to pick out layers within the paint which could give the wood-graining more depth.

Using back-light and bounce off a white floor to light a clear Perspex set without losing definition (Romeo and Juliet; *student designers: Ben Fry and Kisha Miller).*

Photographing models is not easy; the main reason is scale, the sizes of the camera and of the lights in relation to the model make accurate representation difficult. To shoot close detail means having to use the camera on telephoto or macro settings. These close the aperture down, reducing the depth of field and creating a tight focus on a specific item, but sending other areas in the foreground or background out of focus. When using a wide-angle setting, the aperture is fully open but may create a 'fish-eye' effect, where the whole set is in focus but the verticals become bowed. These may be difficult to avoid, but being aware of them may make compromises between focal lengths a possibility.

The quality of the camera is all-important; a SLR camera with separate light meters will provide the best images, but its user may need training and experience to produce good quality photography, whereas a mid-range, fully automatic, 35mm camera with telephoto and wide-angle facilities should be less complicated with which to take good model photographs. Make sure that it is possible to turn the automatic flash off on the camera since carefully prepared lighting states will be neutralized by the flash. An even better alternative would be a mid-range, digital camera with at least 3.0 mega pixels and macro capabilities. Digital cameras have several advantages, they have the capacity to store a greater number of shots, exposures can be checked at the time of taking the images, and selection and editing can be done before downloading and processing.

With a 35mm camera use 400–1000 ASA print or transparency film; although more grainy, these films are designed for darker environments and will give the contrast that makes more of dramatic highlights and shadows. Black and white photography (still used extensively for theatre production shots because the contrast and quality can be more dramatic) may also be effective for certain model shots since there is greater opportunity to adjust the look of the image during its developing. When photographing lighting states, colour transparency film will reproduce the quality of the light more accurately.

SETTING UP THE EQUIPMENT FOR PHOTOGRAPHING THE MODEL

Always site the camera on a tripod since the shutter speeds that are necessary for correct exposures make it impossible to hold the camera in the hand.

The position of the lights will depend on the

Taking a light-meter reading from the brightly lit area of the set will mean that the area remains clear and not completely bleached out in the exposure.

Diagram showing an example of the lighting positions that will help to define the space when photographing a scenographic model.

angles and positioning that are required. Clip-on spotlights from interior design stores are a cheap and adequate option. However, limit the choice to three light sources:

A. A low-level wash from the front to one side of the camera; this will front light the whole set. Try the use of a piece of silk in front of the beam to diffuse the light. Increasing the distance between the spot and the silk will lower the light level. Alternatively, use a piece of black paper rolled into an open cone shape and attach it over the front of the lamp; this will focus the light and make it possible to be more directional with the beam.

B. A high-angle directional light to the side or back corner of the model. This can be coloured-up by simply taping a piece of lighting gel just in front of the bulb. It will provide a light that sculpts the space, creating highlights and shadows. Move this around the edge of the model as required by the different states or scenes.

C. A special: this could be a spotlight on a character, light emanating from inside something, or a shaft of light from a doorway or a trap. Use the focusable torch for this light. Add colour in the same way and tape the torch into position.

It may be necessary with certain models or lighting angles to have stands for the lamps if a convenient frame or wall is not available. Use a room that can be darkened to eliminate stray light.

To make sure that the exposure is right for each scene or lighting state, select the areas from which the camera is registering its light readings so that strong highlighted, mid tones and shadowy areas are each individually photographed. Do this by focusing the camera on the particular light quality, depressing the shutter button halfway to register the exposure and then realigning to the required image and depressing the button fully to take the shot. When having films processed and printed, ask the processing company to print off some sample exposures since they will be able to vary the colour balance. With digital shots, download the images and then adjust the balance by altering the colour, brightness and contrast before saving the image to file.

11 PLANNING FOR PRESENTATIONS

For a designer, the moment when he or she feels the most nervous and vulnerable is when the time comes to present the work to others. It is so important that the concept and the model make the right impression and all intended information is imparted. The designer is probably tired will have been up most of the previous night adding the finishing touches. It is essential that the final stage should always include comprehensive planning that covers content, layout and performance. It is better to present an unfinished model well than a complete one badly.

CONTENT

The structure of the presentation will vary depending upon which set of people are receiving the information. If it is a one-to-one presentation of a white-card model with a director or a first meeting with other designers, then this will be less formal. This presentation needs to concentrate more on the rationale for the design proposal. The designer/model-maker is offering up the design for comment and input from other creative members of the team. Here, too

Opposite Presenting one of the many scene changes in Mephisto. Designer: Gary Thorne; Assistant designer: Seema Iqbal (pictured).

much information might stifle creative discussion. However, when presenting the finished scenographic model in a production meeting or to the actors for the first time, there is a formality and dissemination of information that the designer needs to understand.

The production team's interests lie more with the structure, size, quality, quantities and the individual details that are specific to their production role. So, when presenting the model, spend the most time on these aspects and keep the articulation of the design process succinct and relevant to the rehearsal and production processes. The actors, however, are often keen to hear how the design concept came about, how it will affect them as individual characters and what statements exist within the design as clues to future development.

Structuring the Content

Spend time planning how to run the presentation so that it has variety and is not one long monologue. It is well known that, after about 10min of being talked at, no matter how keen, an audience's attention will wane. Decide who is going to say what. It can be frustrating if the designer and the director have not agreed beforehand what each is going to cover. They may talk at cross-purposes, or the director, who is often the first to speak, may

White card model presentation where the designer is discussing ideas with the director and lighting designer (Mephisto; designer: Gary Thorne; director: Geoff Coleman; student lighting designer: Andrew Hammond).

cover too much and leave the designer with little to add.

Begin presentations with a brief explanation of how the designer and the director have dramatized the text. What it is within the text that has made them want to design and direct it and what relevance they see that it has for today's audiences. The director and the designer should then go on to explain their working patterns for the rest of the production. Apart from concluding and setting up future meetings, the rest of the time will be allocated to the presentation of the scenographic model and the costume sketches. Let the model do as much of the talking as possible: with digital cameras and the opportunity to use video cameras and projectors, the designer now has the opportunity to remove one of the most nerve-racking and time-consuming aspects of formal presentations – having to present the design scene by scene. Every designer has, at some time, stood, trying to remove and set up each scene with shaking fingers and knocking over items in the model. Now, a designer has the opportunity to:

- reveal close-up elements by relaying images from a video camera to a monitor;

Designer and director discussing how best to present the scenographic model (The Kitchen; designer: Nicholai Hart-Hansen; director: Debbie Seymour).

- photograph each scene beforehand and prepare a computer-generated presentation;
- have each scene printed out and displayed alongside the model;
- give each member of the production team an individual photographic storyboard.

Cue cards can be a lifesaver in a presentation; no matter how well a designer thinks that he or she knows or has rehearsed what to say, there will be moments where a question may send the presenter off on a tangent and important information may get forgotten. Cue cards are also better than an A4 sheet of paper since they can contain either bullet points or small sections of text, which make it easier to find your place in the presentation. Holding on to the cue cards also reduces any nervous gesticulations. Always remember to number the cue cards so that you know that they are in the right order and, if dropped, can easily be put back in sequence.

Remember also to make it personal, and make sure that you cover the specific information needed by the several depart-

ments in a production team. In describing the set mention:

- the entrances and exits that exist;
- the overall sizes of the set;
- the furniture and props list;
- how furniture and properties are to be set;
- colours;
- materials and textures;
- technical requirements and special effects;
- quick-change areas; and
- health and safety issues.

With the actors, the presentation will vary slightly. They are much more likely to have immediate questions, not only about the structures but also about the reason why the particular design concept has evolved. It may be the first day of rehearsals, but each will have a personal response to the text and the character to be portrayed that the director and the designer may now be challenging. The presentation can also focus or launch future enquires and discoveries about each character or the play. Therefore they want to obtain the most they can from this first contact with the model.

*The author removes a section of the scenographic model and brings it to the actors for closer inspection (***The Cosmonaut's Last Message to the Woman He Loved in the Former Soviet Union***).*

LAYOUT

It is important for the designer to check the facilities in the room where the presentation will be given before everyone arrives. This includes catering for any electrical equipment that the designer might bring; giving prior notice could lead to the choice of a more suitable room or simply require the inclusion of a multiway adaptor, rather than the curtailing of the presentation due to the lack of sufficient power points.

Arrive early and give plenty of time to set things up. This will include the layout of the chairs in relation to the model, including the viewing height. Make sure that the model has arrived intact – there may be minor repairs to be made. Set up a sample scene with the front-cloth in, if included in the design, and set up at least one anglepoise lamp to light the model. Arrange any supporting references or storyboards on a board or wall close to the model so that movement between items may be fluid, and avoid the necessity to cross in front of the model.

If the design is for a play with multiple scenes, then organize the staging items and furniture in scene order on a tabletop, making the interchange between scenes more efficient. In preparation for the presentation, make sure that any cloths or flying pieces within the model have broad, mountboard tabs attached to the centre of the supporting bar. On the upstage side of the tab, name the piece together with its corresponding bar number. This will eliminate the possibility of confusion and assist in the manual flying of cloths in or out.

It is likely that the designer will demonstrate the model from behind, so attach a printed list of scenes, including what is required on-stage as an aide-mémoire on the back wall of the model box. Have any references or books that you might wish to refer to during the presentation tabbed with numbers that correspond to the numbers on the cue cards.

The most important thing is to get everything set up at least 15min before the allotted time. This will make it possible to double-check and then relax in the knowledge that all is ready.

All the furniture and props laid out in scene order for quick changeover into the model (The Cosmonaut's Last Message to the Woman He Loved in the Former Soviet Union).

PERFORMANCE

Performance may appear a little overdramatic when describing the act of presenting a model, but, bearing in mind the subject matter and the preparation that has to take place, it seems appropriate. Although not giving a perform-ance in its truest sense, the designer does have to demonstrate the dramatic potential of the design not only by the quality of and the expertise embodied in the model, but also by the manner in which the design proposal is 'sold'.

Making an Impression

Rehearsal is probably the most important aspect to have in mind when planning for presentations. Go through the whole process with another person observing and giving you feedback; alternatively, to record the presentation and play it back can highlight weak spots and body language that may be misleading or annoying.

The designers should never hide themselves away behind a table and the model box or read out their entire presentation. This will portray a nervous approach, probably made more evident by shaking hands. The cue cards will immediately cut out the wobble factor. The designer needs to place him or herself confidently between the model and the audience, making sure that to maintain as much eye contact as possible and moving behind the table only when demonstrating the model. If the designer is fortunate enough to have an assistant designer, then this person can change the scenes, cutting down the

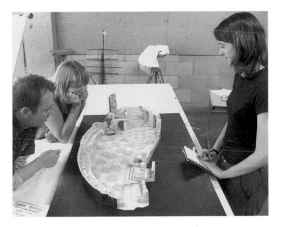

Directors Sally Mackey and Steve Farrier being presented with a finished 1:25-scale model of the Minack Theatre (student model-maker: Eve Lowrie).

amount of time that the model or the table become a physical barrier.

The designer must be enthusiastic about the work. He or she may have been up all night finishing off, but it is necessary to call on every last drop of energy during the presentation. For those few minutes the designer is the showman and first impressions count. Caution or lack of conviction will lead to the 'audience' feeling that the designer is either not completely trusting nor confident that the design is appropriate. Finally, it is important that a designer should learn to value these performances, since a confident and enjoyable experience can truly affect the way that the team and the production develop.

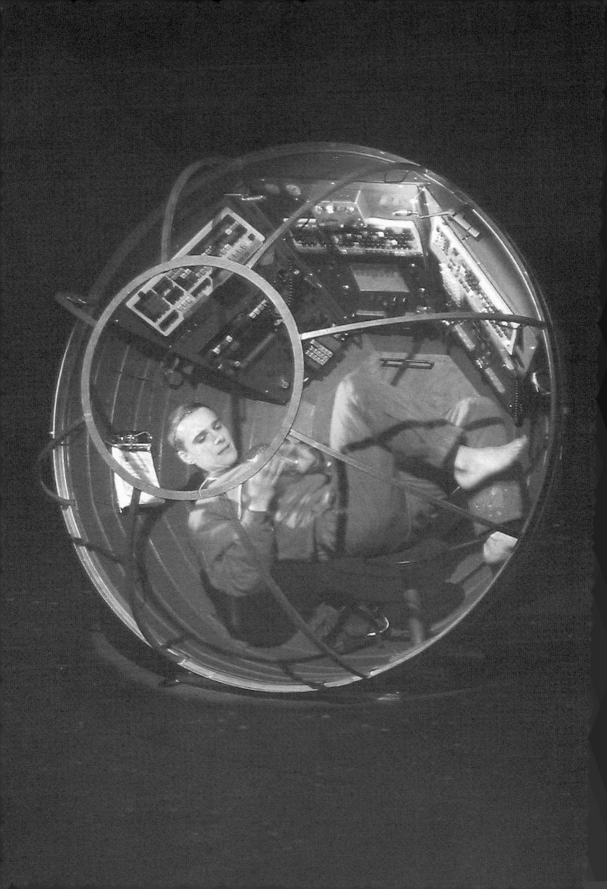

12 PROTECTING THE INTEGRITY OF THE DESIGN

After spending so much time and effort collaborating in the development of a design that is both creative and exciting, it can be frustrating if the production never reaches the full potential shown in the model. How can the designer protect its integrity and make sure that any new ideas that form during the rehearsal period fit with the creative concept?

To some extent, the quality of the finished scenographic model will do this. If the model is accurate and completely encapsulates his or her vision, then the designer can request that the construction and direction should take their lead entirely from the model and the accompanying technical drawings. It can also become a constant form of verification that any further ideas or changes are sympathetic to the design proposal.

However, if the model is sketchy and incomplete and the construction of the set and the use of the space need constant explanation, then uncertainty or presumptions can develop. The focus of the design may be lost or, even worse, be ignored within the direction and plotting of the play, changing its

Opposite *The cosmonaut's space capsule in production* (The Cosmonaut's Last Message to the Woman he Loved in the Former Soviet Union; *director: Geoff Coleman; lighting designer: Lucy Carter; Actor: Jacob Harders*).

emphasis to that of an artistic backdrop rather than a space that the actors fully inhabit.

INTO REHEARSALS

As mentioned previously, the design has a life beyond the model-making. Once rehearsals start, as scenes are blocked the director and the actors have the opportunity to become creative with the space, they begin to take ownership of the designed space. There will, however, be certain limits to their creativity. It is most likely that the construction of the set will have begun before the actors get to work on any scenes. This establishes the necessity to guide the director's and the actors' experimentation so that any new usage of the space is in sympathy with the established design and avoids major changes to aspects of the set already under construction. For example, the rehearsal period is not the time at which to begin moving the position of windows and doors, but the arrangement of chairs and the distances between items of furniture are elements that can remain flexible. The designer must manage this liaison with a great deal of sensitivity so that both the construction team and the actors in rehearsal are allowed the time and space to perform their roles.

Through the collaboration between the designer and the director there should exist a clear understanding of how to use the space. However, in the heat of rehearsal this may momentarily be forgotten and decisions made that lead to unexpected uses of the set or furniture. These might be unsuitable both aesthetically and practically. The rehearsal notes should record these moments, but at times these descriptions can be misleading, incomplete or simply too late. The deputy stage manager (DSM), within the rehearsal, should be the day-to-day link between the director and the designer. To spend extra time making sure that the DSM understands the design and the model fully can be hugely beneficial. He or she can then observe and question intentions as and when the occasions arise, which may avoid wasting valuable rehearsal or construction time.

It is impossible for the model to be in the construction departments and rehearsals at the same time, so certain supporting material can provide supplementary information when the model is unavailable. These are:

- annotated research and references;
- a scenic breakdown; and
- a drawn or photographic, annotated storyboard.

Annotated Research and References

It may be useful to collect important parts of the research, diagrams and drawings of the workings of more complex items of set. Assemble the materials related to each individual item on a single reference board that they can be given to the relevant department as a guide. Add comments to explain how and why the images are important in the making of the prop or the set item.

Scenic Breakdowns

A scenic breakdown is a written list or chart that itemizes the positioning and the removal of items of the set or furniture scene by scene as the production evolves. To begin with, the scenic breakdown is an on-going reminder to

---

Exercise: Creating a Visual Scenic Breakdown

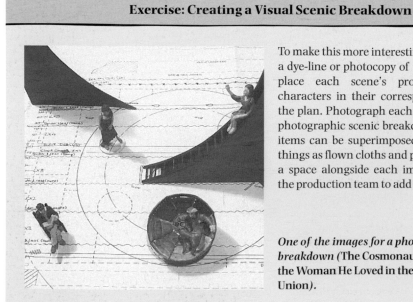

To make this more interesting and relevant, take a dye-line or photocopy of the ground plan and place each scene's props, furniture and characters in their corresponding position on the plan. Photograph each scene and compile a photographic scenic breakdown. Text and extra items can be superimposed to emphasize such things as flown cloths and practical lights. Leave a space alongside each image for members of the production team to add their own notes.

One of the images for a photographic scenic breakdown (The Cosmonaut's Last Message to the Woman He Loved in the Former Soviet Union).

Prop makers consulting a detailed chart of references and diagrams, made to ease the construction and decision-making processes (The Cosmonaut's Last Message to the Woman He Loved in the Former Soviet Union; *prop making students: Tasmin Morley and Eve Lowrie*).

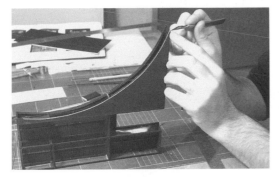

Above   *Planning and making the structure of a model to include the economic use of construction materials* (The Cosmonaut's Last Message to the Woman He Loved in the Former Soviet Union; *model-maker: Ben Woodgate*).

The designer's storyboard image for the final scene of the play; in rehearsals, the staging for this scene was, through necessity, reduced to simply a pint glass and a knife (The Cosmonaut's Last Message to the Woman He Loved in the Former Soviet Union).

the designer/model-maker of what props and furniture are required to expedite the production. This will develop and change during the design process, depending on how the play is interpreted (certain items may be or cut or new ones included). From the final breakdown, the stage management can plan what needs to be hired or made, establish who is setting each item (this may be stage management or the actors, depending on the required aesthetic), and how and where everything is going to be stored off-stage. The DSM will also use it to call in rehearsal props and check that each scene is marked up accurately in the rehearsal room.

The Storyboard

The storyboard is the designer's opportunity to dramatize the whole play visually. Creating a storyboard enables the designer and the director to take their design proposal and work through the play scene-by scene, clarifying how each scene aesthetically addresses the play and provides good opportunities for blocking and direction. A storyboard takes the play in sequence and illustrates the staging, lighting and the movement of the characters. The illustrations are arranged in a similar format to a cartoon strip, showing the entire stage and drawn in an appropriately angled perspective to include the stage floor.

It is important to include all the major entrances and exits and any design moments that have a dramaturgical impact on the way a scene might be rehearsed. Leave room alongside each illustration for annotation; this might take the form of comments that add further explanation of the movement within a scene or directions about the transitions between scenes. The distribution of these, as A4 sheets, to all the production team will make sure that every member of the team has a clear understanding of the design intention.

The storyboard begins in rough draft form during the design process, but an agreed, finished version should be complete with the conclusion of the scenographic model. The form this takes may ether be illustrative renderings or

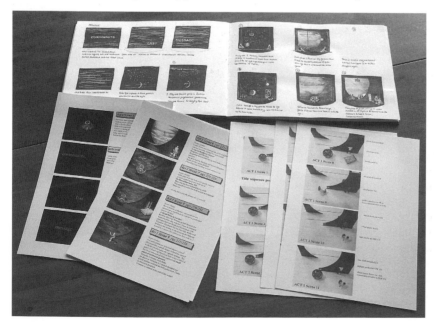

The development of the design concept, from sketchbook storyboard through to the photo-graphic storyboard and scenic breakdown (The Cosmonaut's Last Message to the Woman He Loved in the Former Soviet Union).

photographic depending on the designer's preference or the appropriateness to the particular production. For rendered story-boards, sketch out one perspective drawing of the stage. Photocopy multiples of this and then overlay the characters and the individual scenes with washes of colour and shade to create, not only the position of the actors, but also the qualities of the set and the lighting. For photographic storyboards, create the correct number of scale figures to represent all the characters so that a scene can be 'walked through', marking entrances and exits. Use the techniques explained in chapter 10 to light the model. Set up each scene in the model box and photograph it with a digital camera. Once the images have been downloaded they can be colour-adjusted or have projections or lighting overlaid by using a computer publishing or drawing program. Then draft out the format for the storyboard and drop in the appropriate images to create the finished article, type in necessary annotation or leave sections of the storyboard blank to be hand-written as required.

Actors Charlie McCarthy and Jacob Harders working with the prop maker to establish correct positioning of their sets and instrument panels while the capsule is still under construction (The Cosmonaut's Last Message to the Woman He Loved in the Former Soviet Union; student prop maker: Tasmin Morley).

STAGE MOCK-UPS IN THE REHEARSAL ROOM

If rehearsal props and representations of the staging are brought into the rehearsal process, the actors will develop a greater under-standing and confidence concerning the design and how it relates to them in actuality. The designer should insist, wherever possible, that any complicated levels and treads be mocked-up in the rehearsal room. For complex builds that affect an actor's movement and timing, the designer should talk the actor through the build and, where possible, arrange for him or her to visit the workshop to see the

set in development. This will give a much clearer vision of the structure, which the actor can retain on return to the rehearsal room. If this is left to the fit-up and technical rehearsals, then the staging may throw out the timing, movement and performance that the actors have spent weeks refining. It may even lead to sections of staging being completely cut or not used in the manner intended.

As a designer, try to envisage and pre-empt the sorts of problem that might occur when the construction and rehearsal periods begin. The more information that explains how and why the design is to be used in a particular way, the less likelihood there will be for misconception.

GLOSSARIES

A. ARCHITECTURE

Architectural moulding
Decorative, contoured band that can be applied to walls, ceilings or furniture, made from wood, plaster or stone.

Architrave
Frame made of moulding situated around a door or window opening.

Balcony
Raised area outside a window or door that extends the use of the house into the garden or street, often fitted with a balustrade to protect users.

Baluster
Small, turned column.

Balustrade
Number of balusters arranged in a row and topped by a rail.

Banister
Rail situated above a staircase to provide a handhold when using a staircase.

Box hedging
Squat, clipped hedge bordering ornamental gardens.

Ceiling rose
Ornate, moulded, plaster embellishment, usually with a pendant light or chandelier hanging from it.

Clapboarding
Overlapping, horizontal planking fastened to the outside of a timber-framed building.

Corinthian
Classical architectural order where the columns are usually fluted and topped with ornate capitals decorated in acanthus leaves.

Cornice
Broad, angled moulding positioned where walls join a ceiling.

Crotch figure
Where two pieces cut from the same timber have been set next to each other so that the grain patterning is mirrored in an arch shape.

Dado rail
Moulding at chair-back height that runs around the lower portion of a wall, protecting the wall-covering from damage by furniture.

Doric
Earliest of the classical orders, with plain capitals and columns and lacking in ornamentation.

Fanlight
Small, fan-shaped, glazed window situated above a door.

Finger plates
Small, decorative, rectangular plates, set above a door handle or knob, to protect the surface of the door when closing it.

Finial
Finishing ornament at the top of spires, gables and railings.

148

Flashing
Strip of weatherproofing found on roofs, to bridge any change of angle that occurs; an example would be where roof tiles join a chimney.

Fluting
Vertical grooving that occurs on certain classical columns.

Impost
Carved or ornate block set in a wall to provide support for other structures.

Ionic
A classical order with fluted columns and topped by capitals with scroll-like volutes.

Keystone
Centre stone or block in an arch or vault, usually larger and more decorative that the rest.

Linoleum
Durable floor covering made from cork, wood pulp and linseed oil, backed with strong canvas.

Melamine
Material used for inexpensive furniture, made from chipboard covered in an outer plastic coating.

Mullion
Upright bar dividing a window vertically; made from wood or stone.

Newel post
1. post at the top and the bottom of a staircase that the handrail (banister) is attached to; 2. central post in a spiral staircase.

Parquet flooring
Floor made up of small tiles of hardwood arranged in geometric patterns.

Pediment
1. shallow, angled roof over a portico; 2. triangular-shaped adornment to a door or window.

Periodic capitals
Ornate top sections of classical columns that follow the Corinthian, the Doric, the Ionic, the Tuscan or the Composite order.

Picture rail
Strip of moulding that runs around the top portion of walling; used to hang pictures or mirrors from.

Pilaster
Flattened, classical column that could dress wall, doors or fireplaces.

Pitch of a roof
Angle of a roof.

Portico
Roofed entrance or porch surrounding a front door, usually with supporting columns.

Ridge tiles
Ceramic tiles that run along the top of a roof covering the apex join between the two pitches.

Riser
Vertical face of a step.

Sill
Horizontal ledge that sits at the base of a window.

Skirting board
Flat moulding that runs around the base of a wall.

Spindles
Upright, turned supports positioned between the tread and the handrail on a staircase.

Stucco
1. fine grade plaster painted on to walls or architectural features; 2. term for exterior rendering.

Swag
A fabric drape gathered at both ends and hangs decoratively in a neat curve.

Topiary
Art of clipping hedges and bushes into ornate shapes or fauna.

Tongue and groove
Method of joining planks of timber; one edge of each board has a lip (tongue), the other a groove; the boards fit by inserting the tongue into the groove on another board.

Tread
Horizontal face of a step.

Veneer
Thin slice of hardwood cut and applied in decorative patterns or as a single sheet.

B. Art and Design

Ageing
Process of breaking down a surface to remove the newness.

Aesthetic
Showing a sensitivity to the beauty of a piece of art.

Balance
Sense of equality that exists between visual elements.

Blocking in colour
Where an overall wash of colour is added to the surface being painted.

Composition
Manner in which elements of design are arranged to give a uniformity of style or intent.

Contrast
Where opposing artistic ideas or artefacts are combined.

Crackle glaze
A cracked effect formed when a water-based paint is applied over an oil-based undercoat.

Creative block
Period when a design or idea becomes stuck and there is no clear way to progress

Dynamic expression
Where line is deliberately used to create direction and focus; usually interpreted as movement; it can draw the eye to a specific aspect of the design.

Flogging
Process of slapping a brush against a damp paint treatment to add vertical graining.

Focal point
Specific area that the eye is drawn to; this can be a

deliberate design decision or an inherent quality of the space.

Foreshortening
Showing how an illusion of depth can be created optically over an abridged distance.

Frottage
Rubbing or dabbing of a material such as paper or cotton against wet paint to create a fragmented paint effect.

Glaze
Transparent solution applied to a paint treatment to heighten colour and detail; can be gloss or matt finish.

Gilding
Application of gold or silver leaf to picture frames or furniture.

Horizon line
Fixed line where the sky joins the land or sea; all lines of perspective radiate from this line.

Hue
Qualities that establish why one colour is different from another, involving its shade, tint and brightness.

Linear
Of or in lines; in lines rather than masses.

Mass
A distinct shape or form with weight and volume due to its size, colour, relative value, texture or linear definition.

Naturalism
Style of design that is literal and descriptive of actual experienced locations or things without personal interpretation.

Opaque
An object or paint with a non-transparent quality.

Patina
Result of the natural ageing of surfaces exposed to the elements and everyday use.

Proportion
Correctness of scale between objects in the same space.

Representational
Indicative of a deliberate intention to echo a particular style or movement.

Rhythm
A continuous flow achieved by the repetition of objects or themes.

Symmetry
Balanced visual units creating a tension across a central point or area, usually left to right or up and down.

Tactile
Property of an object or surface arousing the need to touch.

Tint
Shade of a particular colour, created by changing its strength, usually by adding white.

Tone
Variation of colour by changing its brightness through a subtle mix with other colours.

Vanishing point
Point that appears on the line of vision (infinity or horizon) to which the sides of a three-dimensional object are projected.

Wash of colour
Watered-down pigment applied evenly over a large surface area; usually as an initial background colour.

C. MODEL-MAKING

Armature
Metal or wire frame formed to establish the proportion and posture for a sculpted figure.

Contour-lining paste
Shop-bought product usually used for creating leading lines on craft stain glass work; in model-making it can be used to create fine line work or detail since the paste retains its shape and size when it hardens.

Cue cards
Postcard-sized informational aids to assist the designer

as prompts to facilitate a more thorough and organized presentation.

Gesso
A white paste used to prepare surfaces before the application of paint; may also be used as texture for a variety of surface treatments.

Modelling paste
Similar product to gesso, but will create more defined surface textures.

Mitring
Timber or mouldings cut at a 45-degree angle to create right-angled frames.

PVA
Polyvinyl acetate; multi-purpose, water-soluble adhesive.

Parallel motion
Horizontal rule suspended across a drawing board by wires that facilitate an up and down movement to keep the rule at a constant right angle to the board.

Piano wire
A rigid wire of varying gauge; useful because it maintains its straightness until forcefully bent.

Resonance of a space
Term used to describe the inherent properties that a theatre space has and how these might be representational of other locations.

Scenographic model
Final design model fully demonstrating a design proposal in accurate scale, colour and use.

Scoring
Using a compass point to press into but not cut through a surface to leave a fold-line or mark.

Sculpting stand
Tripod stand with a flat, wooden block at the top, adjustable to a required height and rotatable to view a model from different angles.

Sketch model
First experimental models concerned with placing the 'text' into an approximation of the theatre space.

Soldering
Process of joining two metals by using a soldering iron to heat the joint and melt the solder.

Specialist scenic paints
Scenic artists use a particular type of paint that is highly concentrated and available in a wide range of colours; this allows them to mix large quantities and to maintain a good colour match.

Styrofoam
A crafting foam, easily cut with a hot wire or knives to form a rigid, lightweight structure ready for texturing and painting.

Swatchbook
Collection of samples bound together to aid selection and purchasing; in this instance lighting gels.

Technical drawings
Collective description for the drawings prepared by the designer to pass on all the necessary technical information to the production team; they include: ground plan; section view and third-angle projection drawing (q.v.) of each item of scenery to be built.

Text analysis
Process of reading and analysing a text to draw out all the possible information that might be important to the development of a design.

Third-angle projection drawing
Type of technical drawing that shows the front, side and plan elevations of an item requiring construction; in third-angle projection the side view is drawn next to the front elevation on the same side as it is viewed.

Watercolour pencils
Types of coloured pencil with water-soluble lead which allow for different colouring techniques.

White card model
Intermediate and experimental stage of the design process in which the design exists as white card forms in the fully formed theatre model box.

Working drawings
1. rough drawings that designers undertake during the design process; 2. drawings that the constructors make from the technical drawings that guide the substructure of the build and the ordering of materials.

D. Theatre

Acting area
Stage space where the actors perform.

Arena stage
Acting area either partially or entirely surrounded by the audience.

ASM
Assistant stage manager.

Auditorium
Space beyond the stage area where the audience are housed.

Backdrop or **backcloth**
Stretched cloth attached to a flying bar and spanning the width of the stage; fixed to the floor or containing a sleeve that houses a piece of metal conduit; has a painted scene covering its entire surface.

Backstage
All the areas that exist surrounding the acting area and upstage of the proscenium or audience; dressing rooms and workshops are also described as backstage.

Black box
Describes the type of design that utilizes black borders and legs to mask the space, creating a neutral stage space with multiple entrances and exits.

Blocking
Movement within a scene that an actor is directed to make, then recorded alongside the page in the script.

Boom
Vertical bar used for cross-lighting.

Border
Horizontal cloths or flattage suspended in series (running from downstage to upstage) across the width of the stage that mask the lighting rig; usually used in tandem with legs.

Build period
Time needed to construct and paint scenery.

Centre stage
Area of stage that is central to the set and where the actors have most control.

Cloud projector
Equipment that will project moving clouds on to a cyclorama or stage set.

Constructor
Person who builds the stage scenery.

Counterweight bars
Bars that can carry heavy items of scenery that need to be flown during a production; the counter-weight system counterbalances the weight of the flown scenic element to reduce the energy needed to fly it in or out.

Cross-fade
Where, instead of a sudden snap from one lighting state to the next, the states overlap and create a seamless change.

Cyclorama
Fixed, plain cloth or hard wall to provide a backing to the acting area; it may be front or backlit and may wrap around the to the sides of the stage.

Direction
Director's interaction with the actors.

Dock
Storage area offstage.

Downstage
Acting area nearest to the audience.

Dramatize
To turn a piece of writing into a performance.

Dramaturgy
In-depth analysis of the social and historical background to a text that will have an impact on the way the production is developed; a dramaturge can also be an objective eye when considering how the production will communicate with the audience.

DSM
Deputy stage manager; calls the show from the prompt desk.

Dressing
Decorative elements that have no specific role within the production but furnish and personalize the stage set.

Dress rehearsal
Final, on-stage rehearsal where all elements of the production are run together before the opening night.

Dye-line
Copy of design plans on light-sensitive paper and run through an ammonia processing unit.

Eidophusikon
Fully functional model theatre made and run by Philip De Loutherbourg in the late eighteenth century to demonstrate his design and staging skills.

End-on
Performance where the audience view the stage from a single viewpoint (all facing the stage), either in a single block or a tiered auditorium.

Entrance
1. the place of entry on-stage; 2. the process of entering the acting area.

Experimental studio
Studio theatre space with flexibility in where and how the acting area and the audience are set up.

Exit
1. the place of egress; 2. the process of leaving the acting area.

Fit-up
Period when the staging, lighting and sound are put into the theatre.

Flats/flattage
Flat scenic structures; either wood-covered or canvas-covered frames arranged within a set as vertical walling.

Fly floor
Raised gallery at the side of stage from where the stage crew fly the scenery.

Flying bars
Either counterweight or hemp, these bars are used

to fly items of scenery in and out during a performance.

Flys
Term that describes the space above the acting area where the stage technology is housed.

Fly tower
Section of a theatre above the acting area where the flown items of scenery are stored when not on stage.

Footlights
Row of lanterns in series across the downstage edge of the stage that up-light the actors; 'beyond the footlights' also denotes the auditorium.

Front cloth
A flown, downstage cloth designed either to create an image for an audience to view before the production starts, or a means of covering a scene change upstage of the cloth.

Get-in/get-out
Periods when the entire production is brought in or dismantled and taken out of the theatre venue.

Get-offs
Sets of treads backstage that give the actors and stage crew access to the acting area.

Gobo
A metal cut-out located in front of a lamp to project an image on to the stage.

Ground plan
Plan view of a theatre venue with the design for the set superimposed on to it.

Ground row
Low, vertical strip of scenery (possibly cut-out) that stretches across the width of stage and bridges the gap between the back cloth or cyclorama and the stage floor.

Header
Section of soft or hard masking suspended directly behind the proscenium arch to help mask off the lighting and flying rig.

Hemp bar
Manually-operated flying line (without the aid of a counterweight system) used for flying lightweight scenery and props.

House tabs
Curtains immediately behind the proscenium arch; used in more traditional productions to open and close the show.

In-the-round
Arrangement of the audience surrounding the acting area on four sides.

Iron
Motorized, solid metal curtain providing a fire-break between on-stage and the auditorium.

Lanterns
Theatrical lights.

Legs
Vertical cloths or flattage suspended in series (running from downstage to upstage) on both sides of the stage that mask off-stage areas and provide room for booms or entrances; usually used in tandem with a border.

Lighting gels
Coloured acetate sheets that may be put in frames and positioned in front of lanterns to change the colour of a light beam.

Lighting rig
Designed arrangement of lanterns in the theatre space.

Lighting state
Series of individual lanterns creating a particular effect for a moment within the production.

LX
1. production lighting; 2. the lighting designer.

Mark-up
Transferring the acting space and design from the ground plan on to the rehearsal floor by using differently coloured tapes.

Masking
Solid or material structures that hide off-stage areas from the audience.

Master carpenter
Person in charge of the construction aspects of the scenery.

Masque theatre
Court performances in the seventeenth century with highly inventive and spectacular painted scenery and cloths used to dramatize themes often religious.

Maquette
Prototype model prepared by either prop-makers or puppeteers.

Off-stage
Area of the stage not included in the acting area.

On-stage
Acting area.

OP/opposite prompt
Stage right of the on-stage acting area.

Paint frame
Battened frame to which a scenic cloth can be stretched and then painted.

Plotting session
Period of experimentation by the lighting designer with the lighting rig to create the lighting states for the entire production.

Practicals
Physical lights that appear on the stage, may be suspended, placed on tables or built into the staging.

Preliminary drawings
First sketches by the designer to convey his or her design ideas.

Pre-set lighting state
Lighting established for the audience to view the stage before the production begins (on an open set with no house tabs).

Production manager
Person responsible for the budget, build period, fit-up and technical operations within the production.

Production meetings
Regular meetings when representatives from each department meet the designers and director to discuss progress, budget and changes in the production.

Production process
Time after the design has been completed and leading up to the opening night.

Production team
Collective term for LX, props, scenic art, scenic construction, sound, stage management and wardrobe.

Promenade performance
When the acting area and the auditorium are the same space, where the audience are 'guided' around the space to view the action in different locations, often standing rather than seated.

Prompt desk
Console with communication to the technical crew; where the DSM calls the show (cueing each change from a marked-up copy of the script or score).

Prop-maker
Person who makes or adapts properties specifically requested by the designer.

Props/properties
All on-stage furniture, artefacts and set dressing not part of the structure of the set.

Props list
Detailed list of all furniture and hand props drawn up by stage management from the script and after discussion with the designer.

Proscenium
Open-framed wall dividing the acting area from the auditorium.

PS/prompt side
Stage left of the on-stage acting area.

Quick-change area
Dressing area off-stage for actors to change costumes in when there is no time for them to get to their dressing room.

Returns
1. sections of flattage added at right-angles to legs on

either side of stage that give depth or help to mask the stage; 2. process of returning props and costumes to store or hire companies.

Reveals
Depth given to on-stage scenery to echo the thickness of walls, doorframes, windows or arches.

Sampling
Process of experimentation to obtain the right match with the design.

Scale figure
Figure placed in a model box to represent the character/actor in the same reduced scale as the scenographic model (usually 1:25).

Scenic artist
Person who interprets the design in order to paint or texture the set.

Scenic gauze
Form of open-weave mesh that can be painted on or used to hold together open sections of a cut-cloth.

Section drawing
Technical side-view drawing of the theatre space containing the on-stage heights and drawn position of the set.

Serge
Dense, woollen fabric used to create soft legs and borders; usually black.

Set
1. the designed acting area; 2. process of positioning items on-stage.

Shark's-tooth gauze
Form of scenic gauze used as painted cloths, but, which, with its structured mesh, can become transparent when lit from behind.

Sightlines
From the ends of seating rows; the audience's extreme view of the set and into the wings; these should include the stalls, circle and balcony where appropriate.

Stage left
On-stage, left-hand side of stage looking out to the audience.

Stage management team
Comprising the stage manager, deputy stage manager and assistant stage manager(s).

Stage right
On-stage, right-hand side of stage looking out to the audience.

Staging proposal
Stage design.

Stage space
On-stage space available to house the production.

Stalls
Audience at the same level as the stage.

Strike
Dismantling and clearing the set and technical equipment once the production has finished its run.

Tech
Rehearsal period on-stage when the actors and stage crew slowly work through the technical and problematic aspects of the production.

Thrust
Type of staging where the acting area projects into the auditorium and the audience view the performance on three sides.

Touring
Production that is designed to play in more than one venue.

Transition
Change from one scene to the next.

Traverse
When the acting area runs up the centre of a space and the audience view the action from two opposing sides.

Treads
On-stage term for stairs or steps.

Truck
Mobile platform (usually on castors) that may be manually or mechanically moved around the stage.

Upper circle
Uppermost tier of seating in a proscenium theatre; also known as 'the gods'.

Upstage
Area of stage furthest away from the audience.

Wardrobe
Where costumes are stored; place where particular costumes are made or altered for productions.

Winch bar
Motorized flying bar.

Wings
Two sides of stage where the set ends and off-stage begins.

Production shot of The Cosmonaut's Last Message to the Woman He Loved in the Former Soviet Union; *director: Geoff Coleman; lighting designer: Lucy Carter; actors: Dominic Gerrard, Jacob Harders, Sian Hutchinson, Richard Lynwood, Charlie McCarthy and Saskia Schuck).*

BIBLIOGRAPHY

Calloway, S., *The Elements of Style: An Encyclopedia of Domestic Architectural Details* (Mitchell Beazley, 1991)

Davis, W., List, C. and Forder, N., *Doll's Houses: The Complete Guide to Decorating Techniques* (Little, Brown, 1977)

Eyre, R. and Wright, N., *Changing Stages* (Bloomsbury, 2000)

Fowler, J., 'Theatre Models', an article from *V&A Album No.2* pages 80–86 (Templegate Publishing Ltd in association with the Friends of the V&A). Held in the Theatre Museum archive of The Victoria and Albert Museum

Hobbs, E.W., *Scenic Modelling* (Cassell, 1930)

Howard, P., *What Is Scenography?* (Routledge, 2001)

Payne, D.R., *Theory and Craft of the Scenographic Model* (Southern Illinois University Press, 1985)

Rosenfeld, S., *A Short History of Scene Design in Great Britain* (Basil Blackwell, 1973)

Thomas, T. *Create Your Own Stage Sets* (A. & C. Black, 1985)

Thorne, G., *Stage Design: A Practical Guide* (Crowood, 1999)

INDEX